CRETE

© ADAM EDITIONS-PERGAMOS S.A.
  KATSIMICHA, 190 02, PEANIA-ATTICA
  TEL. 210 6644514-5, FAX. 210 6644512
  e-mail: pergamos@adam-editions.gr

  ISBN 960-500-150-0

TOURIST GUIDE - USEFUL INFORMATION - MAP

CRETE

HERAKLION - LASITHI - RETHYMNON - CHANIA

ADAM EDITIONS

TABLE OF CONTENTS

Crete is a special place, unique in Greece. Here, on this island, so richly endowed by Nature, everything is in abundance: tall, proud mountains, deep, cool gorges, mysterious caves, fertile valleys, lush vegetation, steep cliffs, serene coves, wild seas, calm seas, a gentle climate.
Crete is luxuriant and generous, diverse and multiform. It is an island of contrasts, an amalgam of civilizations.

Crete is ancient, yet so modern.
Traditional, ad yet a pioneer.
So ordinary yet so unusual.
So ceremonious and yet so simple.
And, above all, so human...

The nature and the people of Crete will prove this to you. The sheer joy of living, the blessing of the present day, the happy anticipation of the morrow are the island's heartbeat.
Lying as the island does, on the crossroads of the three ancient continents – Europe, Asia and Africa – it has inherited something from each. From Europe, its cosmopolitan air, from Asia its reserved, traditional character, from Africa its palm trees and the hot breath of the south wind. Situated at the southernmost point of Greece, it is the last outpost of Hellenism, and it seems like a gigantic wall on which the lines of the poet, Costis Palamas, are etched:
...Crete of blood and triumphs.
Standing vigilant against tyrants,
Crete, Crete.

GEOGRAPHY
OF THE ISLAND

Anchored in the sea, on the crossroads of three continents – Europe to the North, Asia to the east and Africa to the south, Crete seems to spread its length like a barrier across the southern Aegean. It lies at a distance of approximately 100 kms from the southernmost tip of the Peloponnese, 175 kms. from the shores of Asia Minor, and 800 kms. from Africa. It is the largest of the Greek islands, and fifth in size among the islands of the Mediterranean, after Sicily, Sardinia, Corsica and Cyprus. Its coasts are washed by the waters of the Cretan Sea on the northern side, by the Libyan Sea on the southern side, by the Karpathian Sea on the eastern side, and on the west by the Myrtoön Sea.

Its maximum length is 260 kms. from the Gramvousa point in the northwest up to the Sideros point in the southeast, while its width varies from 60 kms. (from Stavros point to Lithino Cape) to 12 kms. at the Ierapetra straits (gulf of Mirabello to Ierapetra bay). Its area is 8,261 sq. kms. and, together with the islets of Gavdos and Dia, 8,303 sq. kms. The length of its coastline is 1,046 kms.

Crete is a mountainous island, with three large ranges: the White Mountains or Madares in the western part of the island (highest peak: Pachnes – 2.453 m.), Mt. Ida or Psiloritis in the central part of the island (highest peak: Timios Stavros, 2.456 m.) and Dicte, or Lasithi mountains, which dominates the eastern part of Crete (anonymous peak of 2,148 m.).

Apart from these large ranges, there are also smaller ones and mountains not quite as high: Asterousia or Kofina, connecting Ida with Dicte, Virgiomeno, Toumba, Moutsounas, Selena, all extensions of Dicte, the mountains of Thrypte rising east of the province of Ierapetra, and others.

The Samaria Gorge.

Crete also has a number of plateaus among the mountain peaks. The land, here, is usually fertile and the rainwater which collects in these natural basins during the winter makes these plateaus ideal for agriculture.

The richest plateau is that of Lasithi, which lies between the peaks of Dicte, at a height of approximately 900 m. The peaks of the White Mountains enclose, at a height of 700 m., the Omalos plateau, which figures in many a Cretan folk song, while between the peaks of the Psiloritis lies the Nida plateau, at a height of approximately 1,400 m.

The island's plains are not very wide, but the Cretans also use the gentle slopes of hills and mountains, as well as certain coastal areas, in the shelter of coves, to grow certain types of agricultural products.

The most important of the island's plains are to be found in northern Crete. They are (from west to east): the Kastelli plain in the Kissamos province, the Aghia valley, the Chanea plain, the coastal agricultural lands of Georgioupolis, the Rethymnon valley, the high plains of Monofatsi and Kas-

telli in the prefecture of Herakleion, the coastal plain of Chersonissos–Mallia and the low-lying area of Siteia. Between Ida and the Asteroussia mountains (the southern part), lies the wide Messara plain which, ever since antiquity, supplied the entire island with wheat.

The rivers of Crete are few and unimportant. As the island is so narrow, the torrents that are formed on the mountain–sides do not have far to go before they empty into the sea, and they do not, therefore, have time to develop into rivers.

The limestone earth also contributes to the absorption of much of the surface water and to the formation of karstic scenery.

The main rivers are the Geropotamos river and the Anapodiaris, in the Messara plain, the Tyflos and Kolenis rivers in the Chanea plain, and the Kourtaliotis and Patelis in Siteia.

Apart from some water–holes and a small lake (Kourna) in the Apokoronou province, Crete has no lakes or important springs in its mountains.

A particular characteristic of Crete is the existence of many caves, which were formed as a result of the karstic effects, through the ages, of water on the limestone rocks. Most of these have been known since prehistoric times and were used as places of shelter and of worship, as is proved by the various finds brought to light. The most important of these caves are: the Dictaean Cave (on Mount Dicte near Psychro village), the Idaean Cave (on Mount Ida near the village of Anogheia), the Melidoni Cave in the province of Apokoronou (near the village of the same name), the Cave of Omalos in Chania province (known as the abyss-cave of Tzannes) and the Sendoni Cave in Rethymnon province.

Another particularly interesting phenomenon which is characteristic of the island is the formation of gorges which, starting from the mountains, reach all the way to the sea and cut deeply into the land of Crete. The best–known and the largest is the *Samaria*

Gorge, or *Farangas,* in the Chanea prefecture, which separates the main bulk of the White Mountains from Volakiá. Another gorge, also in the Chanea prefecture, is the *Nimbros or Imbros* Gorge, which separates the White Mountains from the Angathes peak, the gorge called *Lagos tou Katré* and the *Kourtaliotiko* gorge, in the Rethymnon prefecture, between the Kouroupas and the Xero mountains.

The coastline of Crete is very jagged, forming a multitude of smaller or larger bays, creeks, capes, peninsulas. The northern coasts are more abrupt, with varying expanses of sand between the rocks. Those on the southern side are quieter and form sandy bays.

Though Crete is a mountainous island with few low-lying areas, its agricultural production is rich, as a result of the fertility of its soil and its mild climate. The main products are: olives, grapes (table varieties, wine grapes, sultanas), citrus fruit, carobs, aromatic and medicinal herbs, garden produce, bananas, avocados, kiwi fruit etc.

Crete was well-known since antiquity for its cypress forests (Herodotus, I.100). Indeed, it has been recorded that the Pharaohs of Egypt obtained cypress wood from Crete for the construction of their ships.

Today we find cypress forests in the area of Aghios Vassilios in Rethymnon. On the islets of Chryssi and Gavdos there are cedar forests and at Vaï, in the Siteia province, there is the famous palm tree forest with its unique and rare type of palm tree *(Phoenix Theophrastii).*

In the Selinos and Kissamos province of Chanea there are forests of chestnut, oak and fir trees while, in some areas, grows a particular type of plane tree, known as *Platanus, varietas Cretica,* which keeps its leaves all the year round.

In the rocky areas and the forests many grassy plants and bushes grow (laudanum, dictamon, aromatic herbs) and a great variety of wild flowers which give special colour and perfume to the beautiful Cretan landscape.

Deep in the gorges and in the most remote parts of the island, far from human activity and the jarring interventions of science and technology, a rare and rich plant and animal life still survives, extremely worthy of study and interest. We find many indigenous varieties of plants, which only grow on Crete, as well as a kind of wild goat (the kri–kri), the *Capra Aegagrus Cretica,* which today lives only on the White Mountains, in the Samaria Gorge and on the small offshore islets of Aghioi Pantes, Dia and Thodoros.

Animal breeding and fishing occupy an important place in the island's economy. Cretan grazing lands mainly support goats, and the cheeses produced (Cretan gruyère, anthotyros, myzithra) are characterised by their excellent quality and taste. Crete's subsoil is rich in asbestos, gypsum and lignite. However, only lignite is commercially exploited.

The climate is gentle and healthy, with mild winters and hot summers in the coastal areas and plains, while in the mountains the winters are quite harsh.

Administratively, Crete is divided into four prefectures: Herakleion, with Herakleion town as its capital, Lasithi, with Aghios Nikolaos as its capital, Rethymnon, whose capital is the town of the same name, and Chania, with its capital, Chania.

The Cretan people are still closely bound to the fertile land of their island and engage in farming and livestock raising as they have done throughout the centuries.

Right: Peace and arduous labour on the Lasithi plateau.

THE ISLAND'S PAST: 8000 YEARS OF LEGEND AND HISTORY

I. THE LEGENDARY PAST

Legend has bestowed on the Greek island of Crete the privilege of being the birthplace of Zeus , father of the gods. Rhea, his mother, fearing the mania of Cronos, Zeus' father, who "swallowed" his children in order that they might not usurp his power, came to the island, with the help of Gaia and Uranus, and gave birth to her son in a cave. He was reared by Nymphs and, when he grew to manhood, he engaged his father in a fight, emerged victorious, and became king of the heavens.

From the union of Zeus with the princess Europa – whom, according to mythology, Zeus, assuming the form of a bull, had abducted from Phoenicia and brought to Crete – three sons, worthy of their father–god and of their noble mother, were born. They were Minos, Rhadamanthys and Sarpidon.

Minos, the better–known and most honoured of the three, became the powerful, just and wise king of Crete, ruling from his palace in Knossos, and from the important centres of Phaestos and Kydonia. During his reign, Crete developed into a rich sea power, flourished culturally and artistically, and her people lived in peace and justice.

Minos' brother, Rhadamanthys, helped him administer his kingdom, while the third brother, Sarpidon, founded his own kingdom in Lycia.

Other well–known legends are linked with king Minos. One of these, telling of the Minotaur and of the feat of the daring prince of Athens, Theseus, is among the most popular and colourful, and has been handed down for thousands of years from generation to generation.

Europa crosses the sea on the sacred bull. (Mosaic from the Casa Romana on Kos, 3rd C. AD.)

According to the legend, Minos' wife, the queen Pasiphae, prompted by the god Poseidon, who wished to punish her husband, fell in love with a bull. From this unnatural union was born a hideous monster, with the head of a bull on a supernatural, human body — the Minotaur.

Minos confined the bull in the Labyrinth, a maze-like prison under the palace, built by Daedalus. At that time, the city-state of Athens was paying Minos a tribute of seven young men and seven lovely maidens of noble birth, to feed the Minotaur.

It was from this humiliating and horrible tax that the brave Theseus, son of Aegeus, king of Athens, resolved to deliver his city.

He set off with the pitiable shipment of doomed young men and maidens for Minos' Crete, and put into action his plan, which was to kill the terrible beast, to manage to find his way out of the labyrinth and to escape from Crete together with the fourteen young Athenians.

He succeded thanks to the help of Ariadne, daughter of Minos and Pasiphaë, who fell in love with him and offered to help him, after he had promised to marry her and take her away to Athens. Theseus entered the labyrinth and, unrolling the ball of thread which Ariadne had given him, he made his way to the place where the Minotaur was, killed the beast and then, rolling up the ball again, he was able to find his way back out of the labyrinth.

Theseus, with the young people and Ariadne, set off again, on the Athenian trireme, for the journey home. They were so overwhelmed with joy by their deliverance from the Minotaur, however, that they forgot to lower the black sail of mourning from their mast and to hoist the joyful one, as had been agreed with Aegeus before they left. The king sat on a rock at cape Sounion, agonisingly waiting to see his son's ship return. When he saw the black sail from a distance, he believed that the young people, together with his beloved son, had all been lost. He bowed his sad head

and threw himself into the sea and drowned. Since then, this sea has been named after him: the Aegean Sea. Neither did Ariadne's love for Theseus have a happy end. According to another myth, the princess was abandoned by Theseus on the island of Dia on the very night of the consummation of their marriage, while another myth has it that the god Dionysos fell in love with Ariadne and carried her off with him.

The story of Daedalus and Icarus is also linked with Crete and the time when the great king Minos reigned.

Daedalus, a skillful craftsman of the palace and builder of the labyrinth, incurred the wrath of Minos because he had helped the queen in her unlawful affair with the bull.

Wishing to escape from the island together with his son, Icarus, and knowing that king Minos controlled all the sea routes, the idea came to him that only if they could fly like birds would they be able to escape. So, he made two pairs of wings glued together with wax and attached them to his son's back and to his own. During their flight, however, his son was so elated by the height and speed, that he flew ever higher, nearer to the sun. His wings melted in

the heat and he fell and drowned in the sea, which thereafter bore the name of Icarian sea.

Daedalus, flying carefully, was able to reach Sicily. Minos, however, had an inglorious end. He was murdered by the daughters of king Kokalos, while he was in Sicily searching for Daedalus in order to punish him.

These, and many other myths and tales related to them, speak of Crete and lend the island the other-worldly and mysterious aura, which has surrounded it through the millenia of its long history, and which is still felt today.

II. A HISTORICAL OUTLINE

The Neolithic period
(6000–2600 BC)

At some point in the remote past, history takes over from mythology, although the boundaries between them are still somewhat indistinct. The lengthy systematic archaeological research carried out on the island has brought to light information which confirms the existence of life on Crete from the 6th millenium BC (Neolithic period: 6000–2600 BC). The limited number of finds show that neolithic man on Crete, as in the rest of the eastern Mediterranean, used caves as dwelling-places, but also had permanent houses, that he lived on agriculture and animal breeding, buried his dead, used tools made of stone, bone and obsidian from Melos, and utensils made of clay.

The Minoan period
(2600–1100 BC)

The British archaeologist Sir Arthur Evans, who excavated the palace of Minos at Knosssos, was the one who gave the period and the unique civilisation which developed at that time the mythical king's name. The Minoan

civilisation emerged, flourished and decayed within a period of 1500 years which has become known as the Minoan age. It presents three phases, which Evans named Early Minoan (2600–2000 BC), Middle Minoan (2000–1600 BC) and Late Minoan (1600–1100 BC).

The reasons which contributed to the development on the island of the first important European civilisation are:

a. The important geographical position of Crete, between three continents, and its proximity to places where major civilisations had already developed (Egypt, Mesopotamia, Phoenicia, Palestine, Asia Minor).

b. The relative facility of communication between Crete and the surrounding island area (Cycladic civilisation).

c. The fertile land and temperate climate of the island, which were significant factors contributing to the prosperity of its inhabitants.

d. The long years of peace, as a result of which the Cretans were able to pursue pacific occupations, to develop their commerce and to cultivate the arts.

Around the third millenium, the Cretans began to build up their navy and to sail their ships all over the Mediterranean, establishing contacts with their neighbours (Egypt, Syria, Mesopotamia) and with the Cycladic islanders. These contacts contributed to the improvement of the Cretans' standard of living,

of their agricultural methods, and to the perfecting of their everyday utensils, tools and weapons. This was the dawn of the Minoan civilisation.

By 1900 BC, Crete was at the peak of its prosperity. This was when the first palaces at Knossos, Phaestos, Mallia, Archanes, Zacros and Kydonia were built, which indicates that, in Minoan Crete, there were kings in whose hands all powers were concentrated.

During the same period, shipping and commerce flourished, colonies were founded (Melos, Kythera) and commercial exchanges with Cyprus, Egypt and Syria were regular.

The sea power of the Minoans gained great renown and this coincided with a remarkable flourishing of the arts. The absence of any kind of fortification on the island is a sure indication of the peacefulness of the Minoans' lives. Around 1700 BC a great disaster, perhaps the result of a catastrophic earthquake, hit the island, which was laid waste. However, the Minoans soon rebuilt their palaces and homes in grand style.

The period between 1700 and 1450 BC is the most brilliant era of Minoan civilisation. Crete controlled almost the entire Aegean area, as well as many parts of mainland Greece.

Around 1450 BC, however, and while it was at the climax of its power and glory, Crete was struck a new and irreparable

Reproduction of the "Procession" fresco from the palace of Knossos. Archaeological Museum of Herakleion.

blow. This time it was not an earthquake, but the violent eruption of the volcano on the island of Thera, which caused great devastation on the island. This was followed by an invasion of Achaeans who occupied Knossos and imposed their domination. Not very long afterwards, the palace of Knossos was completely destroyed, probably during a conflict between the Achaeans of mainland Greece and those already settled on Crete, out of which the former emerged victorious.

After these events, Minoan civilisation declined, surviving only within the narrow confines of the island itself, until the occupation of Crete by the Dorians around 1100 BC.

Everyday life — religion — art in Minoan Crete

The Minoans belonged to the Mediterannean race. They were short of stature and had slender bodies and dark skin, hair and eyes. The fact that there were many palaces is evidence that Crete was separated administratively into several areas, each with its own ruler. There were no clashes between them, which indicates the possible supremacy of the king of Knossos, who must have been accepted as the overlord.

The greater part of the fertile land was exploited by the royal families, the nobility and officials. It was cultivated by a limited number of slaves. Small arable plots of land also belonged to ordinary citizens who were usually craftsmen (gunsmiths, potters, goldsmiths) who worked in the palace workshops. Many Minoans were sailors and served on the numerous ships with which the kings, chiefly, carried out a profitable trade.

The position of women in Minoan Crete was an important one. The Minoan women took part in public meetings, religious ceremonies, and even athletic contests. Their clothes were striking and their hair was elaborately dressed, as we can see from the frescoes on the palace walls, from decorations on pottery and from statues. The Cretans worshipped female deities related to Nature and fertility. The goddesses were worshipped in specially designated sacred sites, in caves, on mountain tops and out in the open. The sacred symbols and animals of Minoan religion were the bull, the snake, the double horns, the double axe etc.

Religious ceremonies, both numerous and grand, including sacrifices and athletic games with bulls ('taurokathapsia'), were organised at special times by the priesthood, whose head was the king of Knossos.

The Minoans particularly honoured their dead. The tombs that have been excavated are domed and carved chamber tombs. However, simple gaps in the earth, small caves and seaside areas were often used as burial places. The dead were placed on wooden litters or in wooden, clay or stone sarcophagi and funeral gifts — various useful or well–loved objects — were placed by their side. The Minoans initially used a type of writing similar to Egyptian hieroglyphics, where each letter symbolized an animal or object. Later they used the writing known today as "Linear A", made up of simplified figures and, still later, after 1450 BC and the Achaean occupation, a writing called "Linear B". The decipherment of Linear B, in 1952, by Michael Ventris and John Chadwick, proved that at that time the language that was spoken in Knossos was the same (Greek) language spoken by the Achaeans.

The major creation of the Minoans, considered the crowning glory of their civilisation, was their art, distinguished by its originality, elegance and vividness, since most of its themes were taken from everyday life and nature. Through this art we derive information concerning the life, the administration, the daily activities, the religion, religious ceremonials and burial rites of Minoan Crete.

Architecture, in particular, flourished, as we can see from the four large palaces of Knossos, Phaestos, Zacros and Mallia — and to these must be added the royal building of Archanes, the palace of Aghia Triada, the rich mansions of the nobility and landowners, as well as the simple houses of craftsmen and labourers. The frescoes decorating the walls of the palaces and stately homes are worthy of particular mention. When the palaces were rebuilt after 1700 BC, they were deco-

Below: The "Tavrokathapsia" - one of the most remarkable frescoes decorating the palace of Knossos. Worth noting is the participation of women in this contest. Archaeological Museum of Herakleion.
Right: Goddess of the Snakes, a faience figurine. Archaeological Museum of Herakleion.

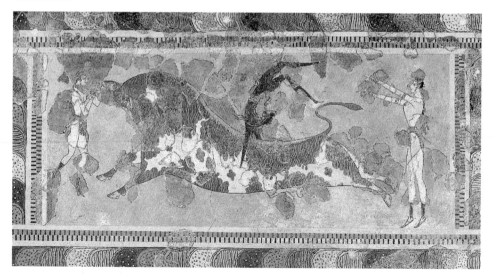

Decorative faience wall tiles representing facades of houses of the Old Palace period. Archaeological Museum of Herakleion.

Tablet in Linear A. Siteia Museum.

rated with magnificent frescoes depicting human forms, landscapes, animals, religious or burial processions, athletic contests, etc. The colours are vivid: red, brick–red, yellow, black, blue and green dominate. Some parts are brought into relief through the use of plaster. The architecture of the tombs is also noteworthy, as are the paintings decorating the sarcophagi.

Another characteristic creation of Minoan art is that of ceramics and pottery painting. The pottery of Kamares — so named by the archaeologists because the first examples were found in the Kamares cave in central Crete — is famous, with its vivid colours and characteristic motifs, its curves and spirals. Finally, small masterpieces have been brought to light of Minoan miniature work, metalwork and goldwork.

Statuettes of faience, steatite, stone, ivory, religious objects, pots, everyday utensils, tools, weapons, seals, gold jewellery, all made with love and meticulous care for detail, show that the Minoan craftsmen were well acquainted with the secrets of their art and served it with utmost skill.

Wide-lipped Kamares vase from Phaestos.
Archaeological Museum of Herakleion.

Left: Flask in the Marine style from
Palaikastro (Archaeological Museum of
Herakleion).
Right: Amphora with papyri (Archaeological
Museum of Herakleion).

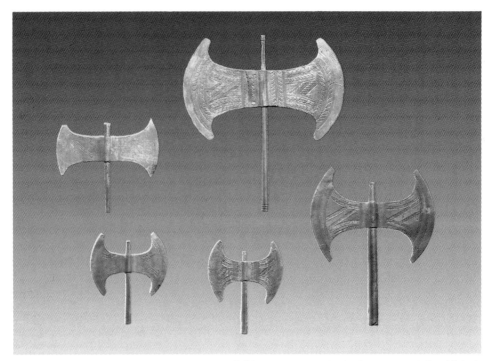

Gold axes (Archaeological Museum of Herakleion).

Clay pyxis with the representation of a lyre-player (1300-1200 BC).
Museum of Chania.

Basket-shaped vessel with double axes, from Pseira (Archaeological Museum of Herakleion).

Marble statue of the goddess Aphrodite holding a bowl, from Gortyn.

From the Dorians to the Romans (1100 BC – 330 AD)

During the period between 1100 BC and 900 BC, Dorians emigrated to Crete from mainland Greece, occupied the entire island and forced the descendants of the Minoans, known as Eteocretans (or "true Cretans") to retire to the mountains, where they continued to retain their customs and traditions for several centuries. The new inhabitants of the island brought with them, not only new customs (burning of the dead, Greek gods etc.), but also the use of iron.

Around 900 BC, city-states began to be founded in Crete following the Greek model, and life was organized, in the Spartan way, obeying purely military discipline. The regime was aristocratic and the legal system very advanced. Irrefutable evidence of this is the famous inscription of Gortyn (6th century BC) – a legal document which laid down the tenets of civil law and which came to light in 1884.

Among the arts, sculpture, metalwork and the fashioning of small objets d' art flourished, influenced by Oriental styles.

Around 500 BC, constant civil wars between the city–states, invasions by various peoples coming from the Helladic area or from Asian shores, and the decline of commercial activity, brought about the gradual decay of Crete.

During the Classical and Hellenistic period (500 BC – 67 BC) Crete fell into oblivion. It did not even participate in the Persian or the Peloponnesian Wars and only later did it take part in the expedition of Alexander the Great, under the Cretan admiral Nearchus. In the 2nd century BC anarchy reigned, as a result of poor administration and civil unrest. The island, exhausted by internal strife, became a lair for pirates from Cilicia, who used its shores as a base for their predatory raids on Roman territory.

This offered the Romans a pretext for launching an attack against the island. Though initially unsuccessful, because the Cretans, faced with external

Above: Archaeological site of Gortyn: Church of St. Titus.
Below: Archaeological site of Gortyn: the Odeon.

danger, joined forces and put up a strong resistance, they were able to fully occupy Crete in 67 BC under the consul Metellus.

The Roman occupation lasted until 330 AD. The Roman governor took up residence in Gortyn, which became the Roman capital of the island.

The Romans influenced but did not change the Greek character of the island in the least. The Greek language, religion, customs and traditions, were preserved unaltered. Latin was only used in the administration, while the grand Roman style of architecture left its mark in splendid amphitheatres, temples, odea, agoras, baths, healing centres (Asclepieia), administrative buildings and various other structures with elaborate mosaics, which are still to be found in many parts of the island. During the Roman period, Christianity was brought to Crete by a disciple of the Apostle Paul, Titus, who founded the first church.

The Byzantines — the Arabs — the Venetians (330 AD–1669 AD)

From 330 AD Crete constituted an eparchy (province) of the Byzantine state, with Gortyn as its capital and with a Byzantine general as its governor.

Until 824 AD it enjoyed a period of prosperity. Christianity was firmly established and many of the early Christian basilicas were built during this period.

In 824 the Saracens occupied the island and set it up as an independent Arab state with Candia (today's Herakleion) as its capital. A strong fortress, surrounded by a deep moat, was built around the town. The name of the town itself is derived from the Arabic "chandak", meaning moat.

NICSIA

Parlo
Codiſinar
glio
Mo
naſe
terte
C.S.tro
C.S. Zuane
Apollona
Mellaho
Ville
Parmilla valle
Aberato
Corazzo
Tentana
di Arana
Niesia
Jaline
Monte
Stellida
Tempio d
Apollo
Tempio di
Baccho
Monte
Pe di Nisia

SANTORINI

Thergia
S. Saluador
Acortini
Scare
Nebrio
Aponome
1 2 3
Ruina
Ruine

SCARPANTO

Fanaria
Faria
ſcopuluſ
Tristanus
C.Cala
mo
Lare
Anchinea
Agata portus
M.Gemali
Scarpant
M.S. Elia
Xanti R.
Corachi R.
S.Lero
Cardamilla
Kenete
Thucche
Alcolfa
Caſſo
S.Theodoro
Plamith
Lersadori

CANDIE

Plana

Petalida
ellagia
S. Lorzi
Freschia Stichiela
Abraba
mirs fi.
Anditriada
Darmata fl.
Piria
Carfelo
Candia
Cachomhore
Carfero
Pian de Balbe
S. Thodoro
Copuila
C. Tibani
Tigani di S. Lorzi
Francus
Milonto
C. Sichia
C. Antelfuhara
Hiera
C. de S. Zuane
Standia
Falconera
Paximada
Paxiemada
Louo
Caruca
Paxi madoe
hea
Dionisodes

Aximo
Catapina
Sifi
S. Zuane
Edelo
Cresonella
S. Nicolo
Salta longa di la
Scoglio di Spira
Muflo
Colochita
Leopetra
Presora
Sirona
Sittia
Serapoli
Iratio
Bauachia
Chiararmiti
Srena trachila
C. S. Sidero
Morena
S. Sidero

Tempio
Philopoli
Monasterio
Territoire de Candie
S. Saluator
Pidiara
Panteon
Mirino
Lascio
Chetina
Carforila
S. Antonio
Campo di Sitti
Pissara
Cogniad
Buco di la
Caco
Pachina
Heliocopoli
Limni
Panorno
Malaura
Vanpot
Cireo
Cortonese
Armeni ust
Siemia R.
Camara
Mauromurij
C. Polio
Grades
C. Palio
Lulachi

Laberinte
Bonifacio
Nesia
Aoara
Mesara
Quesien
natah Matalia
C. Lion
Longo opiso
Coſhna
Mongriana
Arcatina
Rissio castro
Calout
C. Pergamo
Antropoli
Tregiese
Epi Aridoso
S. T.
Fonte
Xeroeamo
Dittee nion
Girapetra
Presistera
S. Antonio
Devante ad
Arcon
Zuziore
S. Nicolo
Do Aretino
Gaiderones
Omal cam
po
nuri
Tasthimoni
Rueto
Verapolo
S. Stroma Crigialo
C. Stroma Crigialo
S. Quaranta
Farioni
Christiana
Menoa
Monte Samon
Sittie
Temple de diane
Cortonese
Xaero
Garubas
Samoni
Sislamo
ni
Cosonisi
C. Xaero

EE

Orien

35

40

20

34

40

20

20   40   54   20   40   55   20   40

20   40   54   20   40   55   20   40

The Greek population was reduced to slavery, while the Arab occupiers were amassing untold wealth from piratical raids into Byzantine provinces and from the slave trade. The Byzantines made several unsuccessful attempts to reconquer the island. Finally, Nicephorus Phocas, who was then a Byzantine general and later became emperor, landed on the island with a strong navy (960 AD) and, after a bloody siege which lasted several months, succeeded in liberating Candia (961).

In the following years and until 1204, the island gradually progressed, the Greek element was strengthened by the arrival of Christians from other Byzantine provinces and conditions became favourable for a cultural revival, for peace, economic progress and social stability.

However, this second Byzantine period in the history of Crete was fated to be cut short by the Fourth Crusade (1204), which overthrew the Byzantine Empire and installed a Latin Emperor in Constantinople. He presented the island to Boniface of Montferrat who sold it to the Venetians for a pittance.

In 1210 the Venetians consolidated their dominion over the island and began to systematically establish a settlement, by bringing over members of the Venetian nobility and military. The Cretans reacted with repeated revolutions and local insurrections. During one of these, the revolutionaries, together with many discontented Venetians, were victorious and declared Crete an independent "Republic of Saint Titus". The Venetians, however, soon reconquered the island.

In the years that followed, the feudal system of the Venetians fell into decay and a new, ambitious bourgeois class emerged, which was very actively involved in trade. The economy thus thrived and the arts and letters flourished.

The town of Candia (present-day Herakleion) - engraving. (Benaki Museum, Athens).

40

The influence of the Italian Renaissance was significant on icon painting, and resulted in the creation of the "Cretan School" — a style of iconography which retained the Byzantine elements but also borrowed others from Italian art. Its representatives are Michael Damaskinos, Theophanes, and Domenikos Theotokopoulos (El Greco) - in the works of his youth.

The Cretan theatre also flourished during the last two centuris of the Venetian period, with Georgios Hortatzis ("Erophile", "Panoria") and Vicenzo Kornaros ("The Sacrifice of Abraham" and "Erotokritos") as its main representatives.

Finally, there are fine examples of Venetian architecture all over the island: great fortifications, ports, churches, monasteries, public buildings, squares, are the work of Venetian architects.

The period of Turkish occupation (1669–1898)

The Turks had made several unsuccessful attempts to invade the island during the latter part of Venetian rule. The most important was that of Khair–ed–Din Barbarossa (1538) who met with the resistance of the town of Can-dia and was forced to abandon the territory he had conquered. In 1645 the Turks landed on Crete and, within a period of two years, had succeeded in taking almost all the strongholds of the island, after which they began the siege of Candia, which lasted 21 years, because of the fierce resistance of both Greeks and Venetians.

Candia finally fell into the hands of the Turks and only the province of Sfakia remained free, though it had to pay a tribute. The Cretans began a guerilla war from the very first years of Turkish rule and organised several unsuccessful revolutions. In 1830 Crete was ceded to Egypt and in 1841 came once again under Turkish rule.

A period of bloody uprisings and revolts of the Cretan people followed, culminating in the revolution of 1895–96. A year later, a unit of the Greek army helped the revolutionaries free several provinces. The island vibrated with the stirring call for union with Greece and, following the intervention of the European Powers, Crete was declared an autonomous Cretan state (1898) with the Greek Prince, George, as its High Commissioner.

A. De Haven. B. Arsenael. C. Niewe Arsenael. D. Ravelyn de la Sabionara. E. Poort Sabionara. F. Plat Bolwerck. G. Bolwerck St. Lucia. H. Bolwerck Piatator.
I. Poort Retima. K. Bolwerck St. Demetrius. L. Bolwerck Schiavo. M. Casteel St. Salvador. N. Casteel St. Demetrius. O. Casteel St. Lucia. P. St. Nicolo. Q. S. Francisco. R. Palays.

I. Peeters excudit.

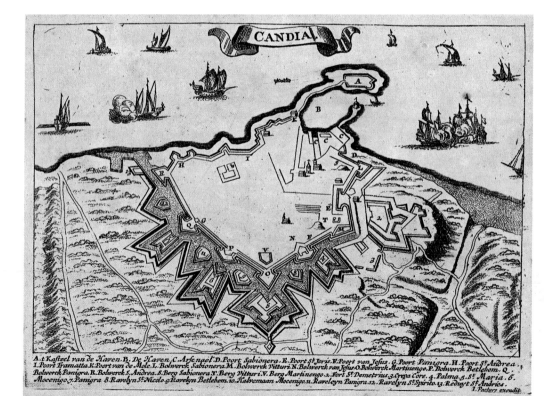

A. 't Kasteel van de Haven. B. De Haven. C. Arsenael. D. Poort Sabionera. E. Poort St. Joris. F. Poort van Jesus. G. Poort Panigra. H. Poort St. Andrea.
I. Poort Tramatta. K. Poort van de Mole. L. Bolwerck Sabionera. M. Bolwerck Vitturi. N. Bolwerck van Jesus. O. Bolwerck Martinengo. P. Bolwerck Betlehem. Q.
Bolwerck Panigra. R. Bolwerck S. Andrea. 8. Berg Sabionera. T. Berg Vitturi. V. Berg Martinengo. 1. Fort St. Demetrius. 2. Crepa Core. 4. Palma. 5. St. Maria. 6.
Mocenigo. 7. Panigra. 8. Ravelyn St. Nicolo. 9. Ravelyn Betlehem. 10. Halvemaan Mocenigo. 11. Ravelyn Panigra. 12. Ravelyn St. Spirito. 13. Rediyt St. Andries.

I. Peeters excudit.

Modern times (1898–to the present)

Union with Greece, which the Cretan people had so ardently longed for, became a reality several years later, after further struggles. The Cretan parliament had repeatedly voted for the union of the island with Greece. In 1905, the revolution of Therissos, led by Eleftherios Venizelos, took place. The revolutionaries forced Prince George to abdicate, abolished the post of High Commissioner and declared union with Greece (1908). The European Powers recalled their forces and, after the end of the Balkan Wars (1912-1913), Union was officially recognized with the signing of the Treaty of London (May 17/30 1913).

From that time on, the island shared the history of free Greece. In 1923, after the Greco-Turkish War and the agreement regarding an exchange of populations, the Muslims in Crete were exchanged with Greek refugees from Asia Minor.

On the 20th of May 1941, the Germans, having overrun the Greek mainland, launched concerted attacks by air and sea on the island. These continued until May 28th, when the German invasion took place. This is known as the Battle of Crete, one of the most heroic chapters in the history of World War II. British, Australian and New Zealand soldiers fought alongside their Greek comrades together with a large part of the civilian population. During the German occupation, the Cretans organised a gallant resistance struggle.

After the end of the war and the withdrawal of the invaders, a period of reconstruction and progress began for the island, so that Crete today is one of the most prosperous and vital parts of Greece in several areas (agriculture, tourism, letters).

Prints depicting Chania, Herakleion, Crete (Benaki Museum, Athens).

THE PEOPLE - THEIR ACTIVITIES AND TRADITIONS

As a result of the geographic position of their island and of its tempestuous history, the Cretans have always been subjected to a variety of influences. This is still true today, if one takes into account the importance of tourism in recent years. However, the particular character of the islanders has not changed. They have always stubbornly retained a passion for independence and freedom, and a deep love for their homeland, a love which has been strengthened by their struggles against the various invaders. They are sociable and warm, hospitable and friendly to strangers, optimistic and open-hearted.

In their daily life they are impulsive and despite foreign influences and models, they retain their customs and traditions, especially in the villages and small towns where, even today, one sees men in the characteristic local "vraka" or long baggy trousers, black fringed kerchief and high boots. The Cretans love dancing and singing. They relish feast days and holidays, weddings and festive gatherings, which in most villages are enjoyed with the same zest and high spirits as of yore. They dance the lively local dances (the "Pendozalis", the "Chaniotikos", the "Sousta" the "Ortses" and others) and sing the lovely "Mantinades", or serenades, with their eloquent rhymes, so full of meaning, to the accompaniment of the characteristic sound of the traditional Cretan lyre.

The population of the island is 505,000 inhabitants, who live, for the most part, in the larger towns of the island. The urban population is involved in commerce and cottage industries, in the developing industrial sector and in the tourist industry, which has played a major role during the last decade in the economic development of the island.

Several factors account for this, among which are Crete's fascinating archaeological sites, mild climate, lovely beaches and clean seas, together with the hospitality of its people and the variety of the landscape. The infrastructure of the island, too, has been developing, and impetus has been given to the construction of high quality hotels and tourist complexes, so that Crete today constitutes a very important tourist centre of international fame.

A fairly large percentage of the inhabitants in the rural areas are involved in agriculture and animal breeding while, in coastal areas, fishing is an important activity.

Special emphasis has been given to modernising work methods and machinery in order to achieve the greatest possible productivity. The processing of agricultural and dairy products and their standardisation involves an important percentage of the workforce.

Traditional activities are still practised by the villagers, however, at the same time as some other form of employment. There are still women who have handlooms in their homes, where they weave their colourful patterns, while others embroider, producing beautiful articles in traditional designs.

The age-old art of pottery is still engaged in, and the potters of today work their supple material with the same dexterity and artistic sense as did their Minoan ancestors.

The grape-harvest in September is an open-air festivity for all to join in. The

There are still women who have handlooms in their homes, where they weave their colourful patterns.

pressing of the grapes follows and, in turn, all the other processes which are necessary in order to turn the must into sweet-tasting wine.

Some Cretans still make their own *raki* or *tsikoudia*, an alcoholic drink, taken in small glasses and swallowed at one gulp. This drink will warm you up and cure you of anything that ails you... It is made of mulberries and is also used as medicinal alcohol in home remedies.

The women in the villages make the local varieties of white goat's cheeses, the "myzithra" and the sweet-smelling "anthotyro", a kind of cream cheese, and use them in various delicious pies.

On the whole, life in Crete today, despite the rapid changes brought about by development and industrialisation, continues to retain its humanity and the serenity of the good old days — especially outside the large urban centres.

At the same time, the towns are vibrant with life, the countryside prospers, the arts, letters and sciences flourish, the cultural level rises steadily. To this, the establishment of a University and Polytechnic Institute in Crete have contributed greatly; there are branches in Herakleion, Rethymnon and Chania

and a Technical College both at Herakleion and Chania.

Cultural activity on the island is intense. It includes exhibitions, plays, concerts, seminars and conferences, which attract a large attendance.

Thus, Cretan culture is re-invigorated and though, today, it may not be able to boast of figures of the stature of the painter Theotokopoulos (El Greco), the writer Kazantzakis or the statesman Eleftherios Venizelos, the terrain is fertile and horizons are open towards a future as creative as the past.

Traditional ceramics workshop.

POPULAR CULTURE AND TRADITIONS

The rich popular culture of Crete which has been handed down and has survived to this day or — as regards some of its forms of expression — up until a century ago, is characterised by a strong and faithful attachment to ancient Greek and Byzantine models, of which it is obviously the natural continuation in time. However, as is only natural, Crete has also been influenced by the peoples who lived on the island for long periods of time. Thus, we see Byzantine churches standing alongside Venetian mansions and, next to them, Turkish structures.

The resemblance of some of the tools and household utensils in use until only a few years ago in the villages, to those of Minoan times that have come to light from excavations, is amazing.

The same also holds true for certain customs and traditions of everyday life which bring to mind what we know of those of centuries ago. For instance, the dead are mourned, even today, in the villages of Crete, in the same way as they used to be in Homer's time.

The culture and traditions of the Cretan people have their source in ancient Greece and have come down to us through the centuries, interspersed with some new elements due to the influence of other peoples, which elements, however, were incorporated into and adapted to the local ways.

CRETAN TRADITIONAL ARCHITECTURE

A noteworthy characteristic of the pattern of settlement on the island is the position of the three main towns (Chania, Rethymnon, Herakleion). They are all on the northern coast — in order to control the Aegean — on sites which have been inhabited since antiquity, so that the chain of habitational development on the island remains unbroken to this day.

Apart from the large towns, the island has many villages and settlements, both permanent and seasonal (the "metochia" or dependencies). The majority of the villages and settlements are situated in mountainous or semi-mountainous areas (up to altitudes of 800 m. and even higher for the metochia).

The houses in the mountain villages are amphitheatrically built on the sides or tops of hills, and thus form natural fortresses to safeguard the village from pirate raids. The amphitheatrical layout of the settlement follows the line of the hill and develops around the church, the square and the coffee-shop. In most cases the houses are built in dense, compact clusters — as is usual in fortress villages where the main concern is protection from pirates — while in others, the houses are free and sparsely built. The village neighbourhoods, harmoniously linked to the environment, are defined by their position along the hillside and, according to their situation, they are distinguished into the "panochori" (upper village), "mesochori" (middle village) and "katochori" (lower village).

Seaside settlements were almost non-existent up to the mid-19th century, owing to the fear of pirate raids, which forced the inhabitants to congregate in large fortified towns or in the interior of the island, in the most inaccessible and naturally fortified sites possible.

After the end of the 19th century, old abandoned Venetian coastal sites began to attract settlers — Aghios Nikolaos (Castel Mirabello), Siteia, Palaeochora (Selino), Panormo (Castel Milopotamo).

Most of the coastal settlements were created in recent years with the development of tourism.

The buildings in these modern settlements are constructed according to modern architectural concepts which attempt to combine comfort with tradition and to harmonise these with the natural environment. Up to a point this aim has been attained, though unfortunately there have been some examples

Frangocastello.

of poor workmanship and arbitrary interventions into the environment.

The Venetians and Turkish invaders have left their mark on the island's architecture. The most important buildings of Cretan Renaissance architecture were constructed between the 15th and the 17th centuries, a period of peace and prosperity for Crete. This style of architecture was influenced by the Western Renaissance style but adapted to the needs of the Cretan way of life and to local conditions.

From the first years of its occupation of Crete, the "most Serene" Republic of Venice, in its desire to secure its valuable possession from potential invaders, felt the need, firstly, to fortify it, and then to adorn it with grand public buildings and sumptuous homes for the officials, thus extending to the occupied island its own splendour and prestige. To achieve this, Venice engaged skilled Italian engineers — the best-known of whom is Michele Sanmicheli — to design and undertake the fortification of Candia — a project which took a full century to complete — as well as the fortification of Rethymnon, the Rethymnon Fortezza, and the fortification of Chania.

Apart from the fundamental need to fortify the main ports, the defense of the island was strengthened by a series of castles (castelli) built at strategic points (Castello of Gramvousa, of Spinalonga, Frangocastello).

The towers of the Venetian feudal lords, which are to be found all over the Cretan countryside, and from which their owners used to keep watch over their lands and vassals, are remarkable examples of Venetian architecture.

If the fortifications, the castelli and the Venetian towers, are indications of power and strength, the palaces, the fountains, the loggias, the clocks, the squares, the monuments in Herakleion, Rethymnon and Chania are indicative of grandeur and magnificence. The Renaissance style of architecture influenced the building style of the houses, the churches and monasteries

(Arkadi Monastery, Aghia Triada Monastery at Akrotiri).

At Rethymnon and Chania there are still Venetian neighbourhoods with town houses, which are among the few surviving examples in Greece.

We also find quite a few castle-houses, villas and rural Venetian homes all over the island. Lastly, the old stone gates, the oil presses, the rural houses with terraced or ordinary roofs are still to be seen in a number of Cretan villages.

The *town house* consists of a ground floor *(katoghi)*, a mezzanine *(metzao)*, and a top floor *(anoghi)*. It usually has an interior courtyard and is built around it in an L shape or in the shape of a Greek Π. It has a covered entrance and the anoghi is directly above it.

In the katoghi were the storage areas and other auxiliary rooms. The metzao was used by the owner as a shop or as business premises, while the anoghi was the main living area of the urban family. It included the sitting-room, the bedrooms or *kameres* and the auxiliary rooms. Characteristic of these houses were the *porteles* or central

doors, and the windows with inscribed or ornamented carved stone frames, the carved stone *koutsounares*, or spouts for the water to run off the flat roofs, the stone staircases and other features.

The *Castles* of the Venetian feudal lords are examples of fortress architecture. They are square, have thick stone walls, are quite tall, and have a ground floor and two upper floors. They have few and small openings and an external stone staircase.

The *rural Cretan house* is simple, built in the shape of a cube, with few openings. The material used for its construction — stone, wood, earth — is not elaborately worked, giving it a plain and austere air, but also one of impermanence. It is perfectly adapted to the environment and becomes one with it, since the grey colour of its stone and of the mountainside on which it is built blend into each other. Later, the Cretans began to whitewash their houses, but also to paint them in various colours — ochre, blue or pink — chiefly in the villages where neoclassical elements prevail.

In its simples form, the house consists of a single room with a terraced roof, within

Examples of Cretan architecture.

*Architectural elements
in local traditional style.*

which all the household functions are concentrated. There is a corner fireplace used for heating and cooking. There is often a sort of loft, used for sleeping, a divan, with the space underneath used for storage. The terrace is built with long wooden boards and, whenever it is necessary to widen it or to lengthen it, a wooden crossbeam is used to give it extra support. In later forms the wooden crossbeam was replaced by a stone semi-circular arch, the *kamara*. Thus is formed the Cretan *kamarospito* (arched house), which we encounter all over the island. The *kamara* divides the house into two areas. As the *kamarospito* develops, another arch is added along the length or width of the house and we thus have the double-arched (or *dikamaro*) house.

In its even more advanced form, other buildings are added on in an L shape, and in its final form the house ends up being a two-storey building.

This type of house is to be found mainly in the *Chora* of Sfakia and in the coastal villages of Sfakia province.

The buildings here are more carefully built, with wooden partitions on the top floor and larger door and window frames painted in bright colours. They are plastered and whitewashed. In the western part of the island, mostly, the houses have tiled roofs and are usually two-storey buildings, with an interior wooden staircase which, on the floor of the *odas*, where the bedrooms are, closes with a trap door.

The courtyard — where there is one — is enclosed by high walls and a characteristic arched outer gate.

The openings are large and have frames of hewn stone — which, on their upper side, have plain stone cornices — for protection from the rain. All these elements, as well as the porous stone which strengthens the corners of the buildings and the arched lintels, betray the strong Venetian influence exerted on the local popular architecture.

During the period of Turkish occupation, the urban house in the towns of Herakleion, Rethymnon, Chania and Siteia was enriched by a new element: a closed wooden balcony, on the top floor, the *"sachnisi"* which, in most cases, has been added on to an older Venetian building.

Among the creations of popular architecture one can include watermills, windmills, factories and ovens.

These, then, are the main types of Cretan houses. Their development, from the most simple to the most complex forms, marks the evolution of social life on the island and can be used as a basis for its study.

Cretan traditional architecture is a part of the social and cultural history of the island and holds great interest. The examples which have survived to our day are very precious and must be preserved at all costs.

A characteristic "sachnisi" (jutting covered balcony) in Rethymnon.

REGIONAL COSTUME

The Cretan man's dress took on several forms, according to the period and local conditions, until — around the late 16th century — the well-known *vraka,* came to be adopted, the baggy trousers common to the entire Aegean, which became established as the main item of the male islander's costume.

We can distinguish the costume into the everyday dress, and that worn on festive occasions, depending on the quality of the material and the ornamentation.

The feast-day costume consists of a navy blue felt vraka *(salvari),* a *meitani* and a waistcoat *(meitanogheleko),* a navy blue and red sash and a white woven shirt. On the head is worn a crushed (or *Sfakiano)* fez with a navy blue tassel hanging on the side, or a black cap, or a black fringed kerchief. High boots are also worn *(stivania)* and *kaltsonia* (silk knitted socks). The chain or *kadena,* worn around the neck with the end tucked into the waist, is an indispensable part of the costume, as is the silver knife, stuck into the belt.

The woman's dress presents several varieties, depending on the region where it is worn *(sartza* in the Sfakia and Anogheia regions, *kouda* in Kritsa, for instance). The most usual type consists of a kind of vraka (*apomesoroucho* or inside clothing) which is tied round the ankles, the *sakofoustano* or sack dress, and the apron or *brostopodia.* On the head is worn a kerchief *(tsemberi)* or, in some places, a little red fez, the *papazi.* Boots are also worn by the women, though these are a little shorter than those of the men.

Cretan traditional costumes are no longer worn in everyday situations. One sees them in folklore festivals, in night clubs and restaurants where folk dances are featured, and in folk art museums and collections. In some villages, the older men and women wear a simplified version of the Cretan dress, based on the vraka for the men and the sakofoustano for the women.

SONGS

Cretan songs can be distinguished into pan-Cretan - those sung all over the island - and regional songs.

Among the first are included the "mantinades", 15-syllable couplets, love songs, but often, also, with a satirical, historical, social content. Their main characteristic is that they are improvised, and this often ends up as a poetic contest between the singers and the lyre-player.

Among the pan-Cretan songs are included the *rimes* which are composed by the rhymesters. They are made up of 15-syllable rhyming verses and tell stories of love, or have a historical or social theme.

Among the regional songs are the *"rizitika",* sung in western Crete. They are thus called because they originate from the foot or "roots" ("rizes") of the White Mountains.

There are two types or rizitika: the "table" songs *(tragoudia tis tavlas)* and the "songs of the road" *(tragoudia tis stratas).*

The former are sung in the manner of the Byzantine chanters, without the accompaniment of instruments, on joyful occasions, with the singers seated around the table. The latter type are sung with instruments on the road ("strata"), for instance when going to fetch the bride from her home.

In Crete one can also hear local versions of Panhellenic songs sung in the local

Young Cretans still dance the traditional dances.

dialect: they are the "akritika" or border songs, songs with a historic theme, songs of the Nether World, etc. Also popular and often sung are excerpts from the famous romantic poem of the 12th century, *Erotokritos*, and from other works of Cretan literature.

THE CRETAN FOLK DANCE

Music, dance, song, indissolubly linked, are vital expressive means for the Cretan, ways of giving vent to his explosive temperament. Through dancing, in particular, which has penetrated deeply into the social life of the land ever since ancient times, the Cretan people manifest their gallantry and generosity of heart, their love for life, and their proud and independent character.

The traditional Cretan dances have their roots in antiquity and are considered a development of the labyrinth dance, a dance of worship, which Theseus brought back to mainland Greece, where it was danced in commemoration of his victory over the Minotaur. The twists and turns of this dance were reminiscent of the convolutions of the labyrinth.

Today, dance groups and associations, on Crete and all over Greece, keep the memories alive and do not allow this precious part of Cretan life to be lost. Thus, five basic dances with local variations have been preserved and are still danced today:

a. The "Siganos" (or "quiet" dance): it is also called "Theseus' dance". It is danced by men and women with their arms intertwined at shoulder level, as an introduction to the "Pendozalis". Its steps are similar to those of the pendozalis, but they are quiet, gentle and are accompanied by the almost whispering sounds of the Cretan "lyra" and the lute. The dancer leading the dance appears to be pulling behind him the tightly knit human chain, in an effort to lead it out of the Labyrinth to safety.

Cretan bread, decorated in traditional style ("ploumato").

b. The **"Pendozalis"** gets its name from the five basic steps, the "zala" as the Cretans call them, which, repeated, become ten. It is danced in an open circle by men and women with their arms extended and placed on each others' shoulders. It is a spirited, bouncing, war dance, which shows off the dancers' dash and gives the leading dancer the opportunity to perform many improvisations and spectacular jumps and leaps to the accompaniment of the lively sound of the "vrontolyra" (a kind of lyre) and the lute.

c. The **"Syrtos"**, also called the "Chaniotikos". It is danced all over Greece and in Crete there is a local variation. The dancers, men and women, dance in an open circle, linking arms at shoulder level. The steps are slow, the movements simple, uniform and controlled.

d. The **"Kastrinos"**: This dance owes its name to the Great Castle or "Kastro", the castle of Herakleion. It is also called "pidiktos" or "bouncing" dance because of the nervous jumps and the light and airy figures, and also "Maleviziotikos", from the province of the same name. It is a men's dance only and is made up of eight steps in the direction of the centre of the circle and another eight backwards.

e. The **"Sousta"**: This dance got its name from the rhythmic springing movement of the body. It is danced by men and women facing each other and is a courting dance. The couple draws together and separates with graceful rhythmic movements. It is made up of six slightly bouncing steps which are repeated to become twelve.

There were also other Cretan dances – the "Apanomeritis", the "Katsibardianos", the "Pyrrhic" dance, etc. which, unfortunately, have long since stopped being danced. They have only been kept alive in the memories of the older folk and in the files of those who study Cretan popular tradition.

FOLK ART

Cretans are famous not only for their prowess in dancing and singing, but also for their artistic nature and their skill in producing beautiful pieces of handicraft. The majority of these objects are destined for everyday use, yet they are fashioned with great love and meticulous care by professionals and amateurs alike, to be used, sold, or simply enjoyed. The women occupy themselves with weaving, embroidery and basketry, while the men are engaged in woodcarving and the fabrication of musical instruments, knives and baskets.

These traditional activities, whether they are carried out by professionals or by amateurs, now involve an ever-dwindling number of people and some of the crafts are, in fact, on the way to extinction.

a. Weaving

In every village house the loom held pride of place. Fabrics hand-woven in Crete are distinguished by their tight weave, the harmony of their colours and the artistry of their decoration.

Red is the dominant colour in hand-woven fabrics, while the decorations are multicoloured. The material used is cotton, wool, flax or silk, depending on the item and its use.

Women used to dye their own yarns, using vegetable dyes – the roots of plants, leaves, flowers, fruits, the bark of trees etc. — or even soot from the fireplace and indigo —

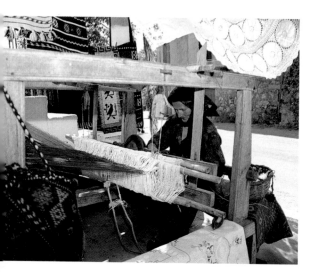

usually employed for the dyeing of the material from which the men's "vraka" is made.

The process of dyeing was complex and demanded much time and experience. It was done by groups of women, who worked, talked and sang together, in the home or courtyard of one or the other while, at the same time, the more experienced ones taught the younger ones the secrets of the art.

The articles woven by the Cretan women were mainly destined for everyday use, articles indispensable for the village household or items of clothing: *"patanies"* and *"chramia"* (blankets, bed coverings), sheets, towels, tablecloths. Also sacks, shouldercloths (multi-coloured cloths which women put on their shoulders to rest their water-jugs on), aprons, swaddling clothes, the men's wide sashes, and many more.

b. Embroidery

Cretan women also used to embroider, and many still do so today. Using tasteful colour combinations and harmonious patterns, they create real works of art. Rethymnon embroidery, with its characteristic "Cretan" or "Rethymnian" stitch, worked with great patience and taste, is particularly renowned.

c. Pottery

The art of working with clay has its roots in Minoan times. Chalepa in Hania was an important centre for pottery, as was Margarites in Rethymnon and Kentri in Ierapetra. The best-known pottery centre, however, was Thrápsano in Herakleion, where the inhabitants had been pot-makers since the time of the Venetians. They used to create large jars, mainly, which are very strongly reminiscent of Minoan jars, and which were used for storing oil. They also made other smaller objects for use in the home (bowls, jugs etc.). Today, there are potters who produce decorative objects.

d. Basket-weaving

With materials which abound on the island, the Cretans – not only the basket-weavers themselves, but also many villagers – wove baskets for various agricultural and household uses: large baskets for carrying grapes after the harvest, wheat-baskets for storing grains, moulds for the curdling of cheeses, bread baskets, and others.

e. Cutlery

At Chania and Herakleion there were many cutlers' workshops, some of which still function today. Cretan traditional knives are well-known for their elegance, their beautiful decoration and their durability. They have a blade made of a single piece of steel with a single cutting edge, a handle made of an animal's horn and a wooden sheath in a leather casing.

In silver knives, the sheath is made of chased silver and decorated with various popular motifs.

f. Wood-carving

The old wood-carvers produced items mainly of religious art. They carved icon screens, icon stands, pulpits, candlesticks and other objects showing an eastern influence, to decorate the churches. One branch of wood-carvers was involved in the creation of popular musical instruments. Today, only a few wood-carvers are still to be found. However, in several regions — mainly in mountainous ones — talented amateurs create small works of art (spoons, forks, wooden stamps for impressing designs on the bread-offerings for the church, lyres, and various other objects).

THE WEDDING

In the villages of Crete, according to traditional family custom, the parents' consent — particulary that of the father — was necessary in order for one to get married. The couple thus usually sought their parents' consent and blessing.

The first step was the "pledge" or engagement ceremony, which took place in the house of the bride-to-be, and was blessed by a priest. After that the marriage contract was drawn up.

Weddings were usually performed on Sundays or other holidays, but never on a Tuesday, a Wednesday or during the month of May. A few days before the wedding, the guests who had been invited sent their "kaniskia" or presents, usually oil, wine, cheese or meat.

Before the ceremony, the trousseau was carried from the house of the bride to the house of the groom where, in most cases, the young couple were to live. This trousseau consisted mainly of handwoven or embroidered articles, sheets, and other household furnishings. It was laden onto horses and was accompanied by relatives and friends in a joyful procession, to the sounds of the lyre, of singing, and the firing of guns.

The religious service was performed according to the church ritual and, following the ceremony, the newly-weds led their guests in the dance in the precinct of the church, to the sound of instruments and bridal songs. The dancing then continued in the newly-weds' home. Before the bride entered, she made the sign of the cross with honey on the lintel and the

doorposts, then she stepped on a ploughshare or a sheepskin and broke a pomegranate on the doorstep. All these were symbolic acts to ensure that the life of the couple would be sweet as honey, strong and productive as the ploughshare, mild as the sheep, fruitful and plentiful as the seeds of the pomegranate. Then the couple sat on the "pasto", a couch decked with flowers and symbolic branches, and their guests sang for them the "pastiká" or songs with which their charms and virtues were extolled. A two-day celebration then followed, involving much eating, drinking and dancing.

Many of the traditions of the Cretan wedding are being revived today in several villages of the island.

For the main religious feast-days or the milestones of social life, Cretan housewives kneaded, baked and decorated, with great care and artistry, special traditional breads. The "Christopsoma" or "Stavropsoma" ("Christ-breads" or "Cross-breads") were the Christmas breads, "avghokouloures" or "Lambrokouloures" (eggrolls or Easter rolls) were the Easter breads, "ftazyma" (seven times leavened) were the breads made for the feast of the Dormition of the Virgin Mary on August 15th.

There were also the wedding breads, the christening breads and others. They were decorated with various motifs made of dough, and thus constitute an interesting form of traditional art.

Wheat, ground in the hand-mill, was used to make the "chondros" which went into many dishes and mainly into the preparation of a kind of soup.

Local olives and cheese, mountain greens as a salad, with a dressing of olive oil and lemon or vinegar, and beans, are never missing from the Cretan table. Among the typical Cretan dishes are snails (or "cochlioi"), meat "ofto" (large chunks of lamb or goat roasted on charcoal), boiled goat, "staka" (made of butter and flour), Sfakia pie (lamb with myzithra cheese cooked in phyllo pastry in the oven), "kaltzounia" (small pies with homemade phyllo pastry, filled with unsalted white cheese and fried in oil).

In the winter months, the diet included sausages and "omathiés" or "tsiladia", a pork jelly.

The food is accompanied by genuine Cretan wine found in different local variations. Another characteristic local drink is "raki" or "tsikoudiá", a strong alcoholic drink made of choice mulberries.

Today, all over the island, one finds tavernas which serve traditional Cretan dishes, "mezédes" (titbits), wine and raki.

TRAVELLING AROUND CRETE

Our tour of the island will begin from its natural gateway and the island's capital, Herakleion, which is also the capital of the province of the same name.

- Some routes may seem long and tiring to the traveller, in particular as a result of detours which are necessary to see certain worthwhile sights which are not on the main roads.
- Depending on one's own interests, one can choose which of these detours to take – or whether one wishes to take one at all. One can also divide a long journey into two, or stay overnight at some place of one's choice (See General Information – Places to stay).
- Travelling can be done by private car, rented vehicle, by taking an organised tour or sometimes by local bus (KTEL). (Information on these buses from the local KTEL offices and from the information offices of the National Tourism Organization).

The famous palace of Knossos in the prefecture of Herakleion.

65

HERAKLEION

The town is linked by air to Athens and Thessaloniki throughout the year, and seasonally to Rhodes, Santorini, Paros, Mykonos and Cyprus. There are also charter flights which link it to many European cities.

The town is linked by sea to the port of Piraeus, to several of the islands of the Cyclades and the Dodecanese, to Cyprus, Italy and Israel.

Local and regional buses run between the town and a variety of destinations, both within the province and beyond.

History

The town is built on the site of the small harbour which was the seaport of Knossos. This small harbour much later became an important fortified town under the Arabs, who held it for a period of over one hundred years (824-961 AD). They built strong walls to protect it and surrounded it with a deep moat (from which it got its name "Chandax" from the Arabic word "khandak" meaning moat). During the period of Venetian

Left: View of the harbour of Herakleion.
Right: Koulés, with the stone-carved Lion of Saint Mark.

rule (1204-1699) it was called Candia, a name which eventually came to cover the entire island. This was a period of prosperity for the town, which was fortified by its occupiers with another strong wall, was adorned with a great number of splendid buildings, fountains, squares and churches, and a time during which the arts and literature also flourished. Then, after 21 years of close siege, the town finally surrendered to its new conquerors who, this time, came from the East: the Turks (1669).

Its name was changed to Megalo Kastro (Great Castle), its fortifications were repaired and additions made, but the town was now plunged into the darkness of slavery, its prosperity was gone, while its population was decimated by savage massacres (1828 and 1898).

In 1913, Herakleion was incorporated into the free Greek State, together with the rest of Crete. During the German occupation its inhabitants organised a brave resistance movement together with the other Cretan patriots.

Visit of the town

Herakleion is a modern town (the largest of the island, with a population of approximately 105,000 inhabitants),

and is the administrative, commercial, industrial and agricultural centre of Crete.

Its spectacular development, during these last decades after the war, resulted in the town's facing, today, all the thorny problems of large modern towns — building anarchy, traffic jams, not enough parks and breathing spaces, neighbourhoods that are becoming impersonal and run-down.

Despite this, however, there are many corners in this busy capital which bring to mind memories of its tempestuous past.

The old port: It is to be found on the left side of the modern port. During the Venetian period, it was an important commercial and military centre.

The Venetian walls: These are the most important fortifications of the Venetian period. Today, seven ramparts still stand, as do two of the four gates: the Chania gate on the western side of the castle precinct, with the winged Lion of St. Mark carved in relief, a carved bust of God Pantocrator and a Greek inscription on its exterior face. On the inside there is a medallion with the bust of God Pantocrator, in relief, and the inscription OMNIPOTENS (the Latin equivalent of Pantocrator); it

is for this reason that this gate was known as the Pantocrator Gate. From this gate, Candia communicated with the whole of western Crete. The New Gate is on the south side of the compound and, as its name implies, it is more recent. It has a decoration, an inscription with the date of its construction (1587) and the name of the "provleptis" (governor), Mocenigo, on its inside face. The space near this gate has been turned into a modern outdoor theatre.

On the southernmost end of the precinct, within the walls, is the rampart of Martinengo and, on a flat hill, the modest grave of Nikos Kazantzakis, with a plaque on which are inscribed the words of the world-famous Cretan writer: "I hope for nothing, I fear nothing, I am free". The view from this spot is magnificent.

The Castle or Koulés: This was built at the entrance of the Venetian port in order to protect it from raids. On its sides can be seen fragments of the carved lions of Saint Mark which used to adorn the wall.

The Castle is open to the public and, on the top, an outdoor theatre has been built. The name Koulés is a Turkish name. The Venetians called it Rocca al Mare.

The Church of St. Titus: St. Titus is the patron saint of the island, and the Church

Nikos Kazantzakis' grave.

The Morosini fountain.

The "Koubés" fountain.

is in the square of the same name. It is a blend of Eastern and Western architectural elements. It was initially built by the Byzantines. After alterations by the Venetians and the Turks — the former used it as a Catholic Cathedral and the latter as a mosque — it was destroyed by the great earthquake of 1856. In 1872 it was rebuilt on its old foundations and later some alterations were made, so that it could again be used as a Greek Orthodox church. This is where the holy relics of St. Titus are kept.
The Church of St. Mark, in Venizelos or Krini square. It was built by the Venetians who dedicated it to their patron saint. After the fall of Herakleion, the Turks turned the church into a mosque, adding on a minaret. In 1956 it was restored to its original aspect. It is used, today, as a Literary Institute, as a permanent exhibition hall for copies of Byzantine frescoes, and as a concert hall.
The Cathedral of St. Minas, in Saint Catherine square. This is a large and impressive church, one of the largest in Greece. It is cruciform with four straight pillars, an impressive dome and two very tall belltowers. At its northwestern corner stands the old church of Saint Minas and of the Presentation to the Temple.
The Loggia: a rectangular, two-storey building, the most elegant of the Venetian buildings of the town. Today it houses the Town Hall. It was built between 1626-1628 by the General Provleptis, Francesco Morosini, to whom we owe the fountain of the same name. During the Venetian period, it was a place of meeting and recreation for the nobility. From its balconies, the Duke used to address the people or view various ceremonies. The building of today is a restoration of the old building, which was destroyed.
The Morosini fountain: It is in the middle of Venizelos square, which is also called Krini ("fountain") square. This square was a version in miniature of the square of Saint Mark, in Venice, and constituted the

centre of Venetian Candia. Here stood impressive administrative buildings as well as the Duke's palace (Palazzo Ducale), and it was, of course, adorned in keeping with its purpose and importance.

Water for the fountain was brought here through the aqueduct, which was also built during the time of Morosini.

Today, the fountain has a central basin, resting on the backs of four lions. The water pours into eight intercommunicating basins decorated whith reliefs depicting scenes from Greek mythology. Initially, a giant statue of the god Poseidon with a trident in his hand, stood in the middle of the fountain, which is why it was called "Fountain of the Giant" (Tsigante). This statue was probably destroyed in an earthquake.

The Bembo fountain in Kornaros square. This is the oldest fountain to have survived. It got its name from the Venetian, Bembo, who built it in 1588 and had it decorated with reliefs of Venetian coats of arms and a Roman statue of a headless man set in its wall. Its facade is adorned with pilasters and columns. In the same square, on the site of the church of the Sotiras (Saviour), belonging to the Order of the Augustine monks, which was pulled down, stands a modern sculpture of Erotokritos and Arethusa, heroes of the homonymous poem, written by the famous Cretan poet Vicenzo Kornaros.

The Priuli or Delimarcos fountain was built, according to an inscription, in 1666 by the General Provleptis Antonio Priuli who found a vein of water inside the moat.

The Public Services Building: Here stood the barracks of St. George, built by the Venetians in the 16th century. These were destroyed and rebuilt by the Turks. The old Venetian gate has survived.

The Vikelian Library, on the first floor of the municipal building called "Aktárika". It was founded in 1910 with books donated by Demetrios Vikelas. It contains approximately 80,000 volumes.

The Municipal Market, on "1866" street. This is a picturesque part of the modern Cretan town, a bustling and colourful outdoor market, offering in plenty all kinds of goods — market produce, fruit, dried fruit and nuts, Cretan rolls, herbs, spices, meats, cheeses and souvenirs, decorative objects etc.

Scenes in the Municipal Market.

Clay swing from Aghia Triada.

Unique model of a circular temple from Archanes. Through the opening can be seen a goddess with upraised arms.

MUSEUMS

The Archaeological Museum (1, Xanthoudidou street.

This is one of the most important and richest of Greek museums. Its 20 rooms house a wealth of exhibits originating exclusively from Crete and related to the island's past (from Neolithic to Roman times).

The rooms include, in brief:

Ground floor:

Room I: Neolithic and Pre-palatial Minoan civilization (2500-2000 BC).

Room II: Early Palatial Minoan civilization. Palaces of Knossos, Mallia and Peak Sanctuaries (2000-1700 BC).

Room III: Early Palatial Minoan civilization. Palace of Phaestos (2000-1700 BC).

Room IV: Neo-palatial Minoan civilization. Palaces of Knossos, Phaestos and Mallia (1700-1450 BC).

Room V: advanced and final phase of the Neo-palatial civilization. Palace of Knossos (1450-1400 BC).

Room VI: Neo-palatial and Post-palatial civilization. Necropolis of Knossos and of Phaestos (1400-1350 BC).

Room VII: Neo-palatial Minoan civilization. Mansions, villas, caves of central Crete (1700-1450 BC).

Room VIII: Neo-palatial Minoan civilization. Palace of Zacros (1700-1450 BC).

Room IX: Neo-palatial Minoan civilization. Sites of eastern Crete (1700-1450 BC).

Room X: Post-palatial Minoan civilization (1400-1100 BC).

Room XI: Sub-Minoan and Proto-Geometric civilization (1100-800 BC).

Room XII: Later Geometric civilization with Orientalizing influences (800-650 BC).

Room XIII: Minoan Sarcophagi.

Room XIX: Monumental art of the Archaic period (7th and 6th centuries BC).
Room XX: Greek and Greco-Roman sculpture of the 5th century - 4th century BC).

First floor

Room XIV: Neo-palatial Minoan civilization. Frescoes (1600-1400 BC).
Room XV: Neo-palatial Minoan civilization. Frescoes (1600-1400 BC)
Room XVI: Neo-palatial Minoan civilization. Frescoes (1600-1400 BC).
Room XVII: Giamalaki collection.
Room XVIII: Small objects and ornaments of the Archaic, Classical, Hellenistic and Roman periods (7th century – 4th century BC).
Room Z: Scientific collection to aid in the study of Minoan Archaeology.

Frescoes from the palace of Knossos: The Dolphin fresco - The Ladies of the Court - the "Parisienne".

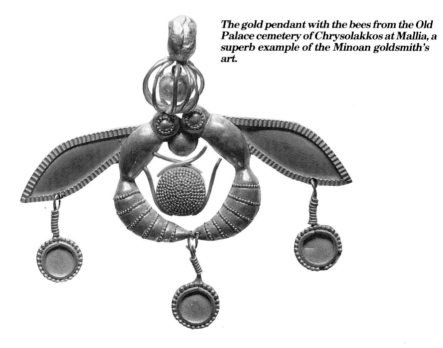

The gold pendant with the bees from the Old Palace cemetery of Chrysolakkos at Mallia, a superb example of the Minoan goldsmith's art.

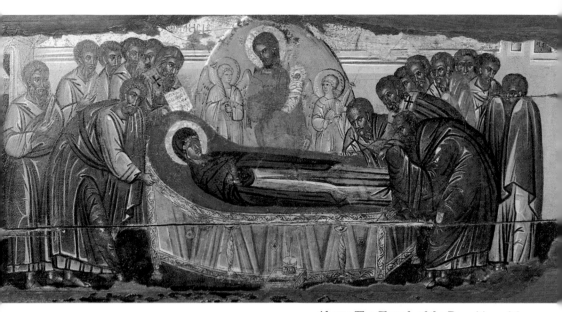

Above: The Church of the Dormition of the Holy Virgin.
Below: The Prophets, from the Panaghia Gouverniotissa Church.

Historic – National Museum (7, Kalokairinou St.)

This museum is housed in a three-storey neoclassical building in the Bendenaki area, belonging to the Kalokairinos family. It was founded in 1953 by the Cretan Society of Historical Studies. In its twelve rooms – thanks to the exhibits displayed in chronological order — the visitor is able to follow the evolution of Cretan civilization in its consistent course, from the early years of Christianity up to the 20th century. It contains sculptures and architectural elements, frescoes, icons, historic relics, documents, maps, books, handicrafts, Cretan folk costumes and jewellery, portraits, firearms belonging to the fighters who took part in the wars of independence, sultans' firmans (royal decrees), as well as objects of everyday use, musical instruments, woodcarved chests. In a separate room on the first floor (the Kazantzaki room) are kept manuscripts, letters and other personal items belonging to the great writer. In the first floor passage there are mediaeval maps, and photographic archives of the period between 1867 and 1912 and of the Battle of Crete.

An arched house, or "kamarospito", in the Historical Museum of Crete.

Room 10, on the second floor, has been turned into a typical rural Cretan house (a "kamaróspito") with its characteristic "kamara", its fireplace, household objects, furniture, a bed all made up, a candlestick and oil lamp, the stand on which the women used to place their water jugs, the family icon-stand, and various kinds of agricultural implements. In the space behind the room is the workshop with all the necessary implements for weaving.

Collection of Byzantine icons – Saint Catherine's church (Aghia Aikaterini square) – also called the Museum of Religious Art.
It is housed in the church of Saint Catherine which is a dependency of Mount Sinai. The church is a basilica with a transverse nave. Its northern side has been turned into a chapel with a cupola (Aghioi Deka). It was built in the 15th century and was turned into a mosque during the Turkish occupation.

It includes important frescoes of the 13th and 14th centuries, Christian relics, manuscripts, religious books, wood–carvings and many Byzantine icons. Six of these, which are particularly important, are attributed to the Cretan painter of the 16th century, Michael Damaskinos, who worked not only in Crete but also in the Ionian islands and in Venice.

The Church of Aghia Aikaterini.

TOURS STARTING FROM HERAKLEION

VISIT TO KNOSSOS

The archaeological site of Knossos is at a distance of 5 kms. southeast of Herakleion, near the small village of the same name, on a hill. A local bus (No 2) runs very regulary between Herakleion and Knossos and all the tourist agencies organise visits and guided tours to the site.

The name Knossos is mentioned in the Minoan tablets in Linear B. It is by this name that it is mentioned by Homer, who speaks of Knossos as a big city. Strabo also considers Knossos and Gortyn the greatest and most powerful cities in Crete. Its perimeter was said to have measured 30 stadia (stadium: a unit of length equal to 606.95 English feet) and its population, at the time of its peak, numbered 100,000 inhabitants. The cemeteries which were found in the surrounding area, east and west of the palace, confirm this information. In particular, on the hill of Saint Elijah (Aï–Liás), east of the palace, a Minoan grave was discovered, while in 1980, in the Aï–Yiannis suburb (west of Knossos), an Early Geometric hewn grave was found, containing cups, ornamental pins etc. Also, at a site west of the palace, another grave was discovered which, however, had been plundered.

The first palace of Knossos was built around 1900 BC, on the remains of a pre–existing Neolithic settlement, which had been inhabited since 6000 BC. This palace was destroyed around 1700 BC and, in its place, another one was built. During the period between

Palace of Knossos. The northern side of the Central Court.

1700–1450 BC, Minoan Crete, and especially Knossos, was at the height of its brilliance and power. In 1600, a destructive earthquake caused serious damage. Soon, however, the necessary repairs were made and, at the same time, other sumptuous buildings were erected on the same site. Around 1450, a new catastrophe occurred — probably due to the eruption of the volcano on Thera — with destructive effects.

Then came the invasion of the Achaeans and, a little later, during a battle, the palace was totally destroyed. After this, the palace area was no longer used, but Knossos continued to be an important city–state until the first Byzantine period.

During the Roman period, Gortyn was established as the most important town of the island and was the seat of the Praetorians, Knossos taking second place.

During the Venetian period, Knossos sank into oblivion, its glorious name was forgotten, and it was only mentioned thereafter, and until not so long ago, as "Makrytoichos" (Long Walls). It was now only a small settlement built on the Roman ruins, which got its name from a long wall, surviving from Roman Knossos.

Almost all the ruins of the palace which have survived today, belong to the Neo–palatial period.

In 1878, Minos Kalokairinos, a citizen of Herakleion fired with a great love for antiquity began, on his own private initiative, the first trial excavations on the Knossos hill - a site which, at that

81

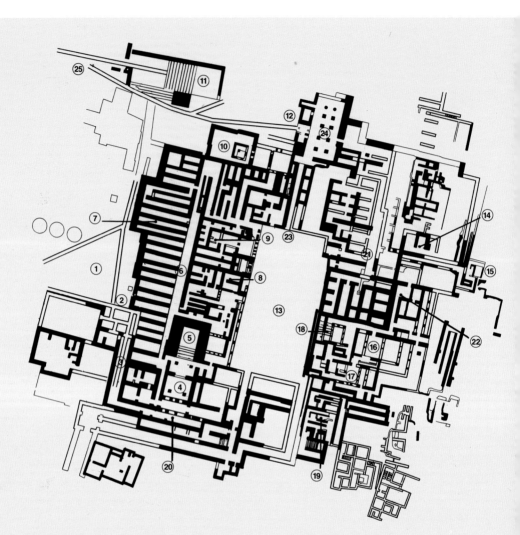

KNOSSOS - PLAN OF THE GREAT PALACE

1. WEST COURT
2. WEST ENTRANCE
3. CORRIDOR OF THE PROCESSION
4. PROPYLAEA
5. STAIRWAY
6. CORRIDOR OF THE STOREROOMS
7. STOREROOMS
8. SANCTUARY
9. THRONE ROOM
10. LUSTRAL BASIN
11. OUTDOOR THEATRE
12. NORTH ENTRANCE
13. CENTRAL COURT

14. STOREROOMS WITH PITHOI
15. EAST BASTION
16. HALL OF THE DOUBLE AXES
17. QUEEN'S "MEGARON" (APARTMENTS)
18. GRAND STAIRCASE
19. SMALL SANCTUARY OF THE DOUBLE AXES
20. SOUTH ENTRANCE
21. CORRIDOR OF THE DRAUGHTBOARD
22. WORKSHOPS
23. NORTH CORRIDOR
24. CUSTOMS HOUSE
25. PAVED WAY TO THE LITTLE PALACE

The southern Propylaea of the palace, with the sacred double horns.

time, was covered by arable land. He uncovered a number of large jars and other objects, but soon gave up his excavations. Systematic excavations of the site were begun in 1900 by the British archaeologist, Sir Arthur Evans, and his collaborators. The excavations were carried on intermittently for 35 years. Evans has left us an important collection of writings on his excavations of Knossos. They consist of four volumes (*The Palace of Minos,* ed. 1921–1935), and a great many reports. The reconstruction of the palace of Knossos, executed by Evans, was considered by many too ostentatious and overdone, and he was criticized for using too much reinforced concrete. Despite this, however, it was later seen that the multi–storey buildings would not have been able to stand up to time if they had not been sustained in this way.

In the following pages, a brief description is given of the most important buildings of the archaeological site of Knossos. Visitors are only allowed access to the Great Palace, the Minoan

houses around it and the house of the Archpriest.

I. The Great Palace

In order to grasp the grandeur of this palace, we must imagine that it covered the entire hill (an area of 20,000 sq. metres), that some parts of the building were five storeys high and that it had a total number of 1400 rooms. The visitor of today will admire the good use of space — achieved by taking advantage of the various levels of the hill – the perfect lighting, which was attained through the use of colonnades and interior courtyards, the functional design and especially the aesthetic value of this grand restored edifice. Each part of the palace had a special use: in the western part were concentrated the ceremonial apartments, the administrative area, as well as the public storerooms. This section also housed the famous Throne Room.

On the eastern side were the private rooms of the palace (the royal apartments, the attendants' quarters, wash-

Storerooms with jars.

rooms etc.). To the north of the royal apartments were the workshops of the various craftsmen employed in the king's service, and the royal storerooms.

The visitor today enters the palace through the *western courtyard.* In the southeastern corner of the court is the *western entrance,* which leads to the so–called *Corridor of the Procession,* which owes its name to the fresco of the Procession which decorated the walls and which today is exhibited in the Archaeological Museum in Herakleion. To the left of the corridor are the *Propylaea* (outer entrance) of the palace. Here, on a special stand of the Propylaea, are set the huge *double horns—* the sacred symbol of the Minoan religion — which adorn the opening of the corridor wall. A stairway leads to the top floor and another smaller one to the *central court.* On the northwestern side of the court is the *Throne Room,* which consists of an antechamber and the main room. In the anteroom there is a reproduction in wood of the throne in the next room, stone benches and a sunken "lustral area". In the main room there is the stone throne and

benches made of gypsum. On the walls are painted figures of griffins, symbolizing the strength of the king of Knossos (copy of the original painting which can be seen in the Herakleion Archaeological Museum). This area served as a kind of Consistory where the Archpriest–Judge–King passed judgement, sitting on his simple but imposing throne, while his counsellors sat on the surrounding benches. Next to the antechamber of the Throne Room is the stairway leading to the top floor, to the halls where ceremonies were held and to the *sanctuary with the three pillars* and square piers.

Next to the base of the stairway is the central sanctuary of the palace. It includes the *antechamber of the Crypts* with the square piers, on which the double–axe is inscribed, the *room of the Giant Pithoi* and the *treasury* of the sanctuary, where precious objects were found, among which the "goddesses of the snakes", faience statuettes dating from around 1600 BC, which can be seen in the Herakleion Archaeological Museum.

Near the southwestern corner of the central court the Corridor of the Procession ends. This is where the *"prince with the lilies"* was found, a fresco showing a young man in relief with a wreath of flowers and peacock feathers on his head, who is leading a sacred animal. The original is exhibited in the Herakleion Archaeological Museum, and in the place where the original was discovered, we can now see a reproduction.

At the back of the west side, perpendicularly to the *corridor of the storerooms,* were built the eighteen long and narrow *storerooms* containing the bulky jars where the year's harvest was kept.

Almost in the centre of the eastern side of the central court is the *great stairway.* This leads to the eastern wing of the palace which houses the royal apartments. Further to the east is the *room of the double axes,* which communicates with the main hall of the royal palace. A hallway leads to the

The anteroom to the Throne Room.

The imposing Throne Room.

Left: The Queen's apartments (above).
The colonnade of the Grand Staircase
(below).

queen's apartments. Here, on the section of the wall above the entrance, we can see a copy of the *Dolphin fresco* (the original of which is in the Archaeological Museum of Herakleion).

To the west of the queen's apartments towards the central court are small rooms which were the queen's bathroom and boudoir, which were fitted with a system of running water and drains.

To the northeast of the queen's apartments are the *royal storerooms* and next to these is the *corridor of the draughtboard,* which got its name from the inlaid gaming table which was found here (now in the Herakleion Museum). To the south of the storerooms are the various workshops. Another corridor, parallel to the Corridor of the Draughtboard, bearing north, is the *northern corridor* leading out of the palace. At the point where it comes to an end, there is a rectangular room with columns and square piers, known as the *Customs House.* Outside the palace, on the northern corner, is the *lustral area* and, to the northwest of this, we find the *Theatre.* It is a flat, paved area with tiers of steps on two sides and a square platform on the side of the Palace, which is believed to have been King Minos' royal box. From the theatre, a small paved road leads to the Little Palace.

The West wing of the palace.

II. The Little Palace

To the northwest of the main palace, we find the second largest building of the archaeological site of Knossos. It is a two-storey building with a paved interior court. In a room on the southwestern corner was found a depository containing ritual vessels, among which the cup with the wonderful bull's head in steatite which is today exhibited in the Herakleion Archaeological Museum.

VI. The Royal Temple Tomb

This lies about one kilometre south of the palace and was linked to the High Priest's House by a paved road. It seems to have been the tomb of one of the last kings of Knossos.

It is a two–storey structure with a pillar crypt carved out of the rock. The upper floor was believed to have served as a shrine for the worship of the dead.

In the area of "Ariadne's Villa" is located the Stratigraphic Museum containing a stratigraphic collection from the excavations of the site.

VII. House of Dionysus

To the right of the road leading to the archaeological site of Knossos, and just before we get to it, lies the Roman House of Dionysus, which dates from the time of the Roman emperor, Hadrian (76–138 AD). It owes its name to the wonderful mosaic floors with themes inspired by the myths related to the god Dionysus.

III. The Royal Villa

This is to the northeast of the Great Palace and is considered to be one of the Palace's dependencies. It is a two–storey building and belongs to the end of the Neo–palatial period, as does the Little Palace.

At the far end of the villa, in a recess in the wall, stood the throne. There was a space for sacrifices and an imposing staircase. In the royal villa was found a gigantic jar decorated with a painting in relief depicting clumps of papyrus.

IV. The House of the High Priest

This is a Minoan edifice with a stone altar flanked by stands for double axes. It is believed that the area was railed off by a metal grille.

V. The Caravanserai

Opposite the south side of the Great Palace, beyond the ravine, lies this building which, from the findings excavated – fragments of clay bath-tubs — is believed to have been a public bath with running water.

It communicated with the palace by a bridge. Its walls are decorated with a reproduction of a frieze depicting partridges and hoopoes. The original is exhibited in the Herakleion Archaeological Museum.

Reproduction of the central light well.

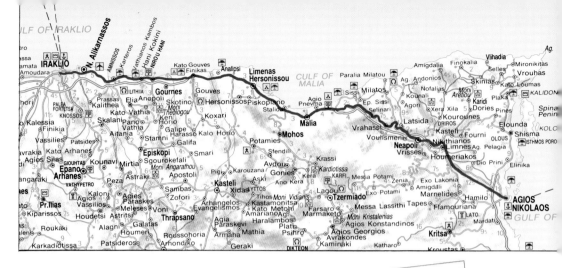

HERAKLEION–
AGHIOS NIKOLAOS

Herakleion – Herakleion Airport – Karteros – Chani Nirou – Limenas Chersonissou – Stalis – Mallia – Selinaris – Vrahassi – Latsida – Neapolis – Aghios Nikolaos.

This route covers a large part of the northeastern axis of the island and links the capitals of the prefectures of Herakleion and Lasithi. All along its length, or after making short detours, one comes across important archaeological sites and many attractive places which offer accommodation and amenities to the tourist.

One can take either the old national road or the shorter new national road.

In our description, we shall follow the old road which, in its major portion, runs along the coast, moving inland after Mallia and, a little further to the west, running southeastwards towards Neapolis and Aghios Nikolaos. On the way out of Herakleion, after the suburb of *Nea Alikarnassos,* we pass the airport of *Herakleion.* At the 7th km. to the left lies the organised beach of *Karteros.* From here, we can distinguish, in the Cretan sea, the islet of Dia and, very soon afterwards, we come upon *Amnissos,* the harbour of Minoan Knossos, which was built around the Palaeochora hill. Here, during the excavations under Professor Marinatos, a Minoan villa dating from approximately 1600 BC, known as the *"Villa of the Amnissos Frescoes",* was brought to light.

Left: View of Limenas Chersonisou
Above: Amnisos,
the wall-painting of the lilies.

This villa has an area of 20x20 metres and consists of a ground floor and an upper floor. In one of the upper floor rooms were found the *frescoes with the lilies,* a work showing an extraordinary mastery of technique with the stems and flowers of the plant impressed. They are exhibited in the Herakleion Archaeological Museum. During the excavations, ruins of a building were also brought to light, which was given the name of the "Harbour–master's Office", as well as a limestone wall, steps — believed to have been rows of seats in a theatre — and an outdoor sanctuary with a large circular altar. On the crest of the same hill was built the Venetian village of Mesovouni.

As we continue to the east, we pass the valley of *Vathi* and find ourselves in the archaeological area of *Niros,* (15 kms.) also known as *"Chani tou Nirou"* or *"Chani Kokkini"* from the name of the settlement which exists there.

On this spot, in 1918, S. Xanthoudides excavated a most important and very well-preserved *Minoan villa.*

It appears to have been the house of the overlord, and this is why it was called the "House of the High Priest."

Among the findings on the site were many ritual objects. One kilometre west of the villa, at a spot called Aghioi Theodoroi, the remains of a Minoan dockyard and a port were found, belonging to Knossos, the ruler of the seas.

Further along we come to *Kato Gournes,* and at the 23rd km, a road to the right leads to the Lasithi plateau (see route 3). At the 26th km. is *Limenas Chersonissou,* on the western point of Mallia Bay, a busy tourist centre with many large hotels, shops, restaurants, tavernas etc.

As the remains of a Minoan settlement west of the town indicate, this place had been inhabited since Minoan times. Later, according to the geographer and historian Strabo, it was used as a port for Lyttos. During Roman and early Byzantine times, the town flourished. It was an important town and was supplied with water by means of a Roman aqueduct (of the 1st or 2nd century AD), ruins of which survive at the site called Xerokamáres, to the northwest of Potamiés village.

Our route, following the curve of the bay, continues to the southeast and passing through *Stalis* (at the 30.5 km) and Mallia (34.5 km) lovely beaches with tourist accommodations and shops, arrives at the archaeological site of *Mallia,* 3 kms. east of the modern town of the same name. At the 31.5 kilometre, a road to the right leads to Mochos and to the Lasithi plateau (see route 3).

Left above: Anisaras.
Left below: Gouves.
Right below: Stalis.

Pp. 94-95: Limenas Chersonisou
-a well-equipped seaside resort very popular with tourists.

Visit of Mallia

Mallia was an important Minoan town with a palace equivalent in size to those of Knossos and Phaestos, but not so grand.

Here, no frescoes were found, nor Kamares pots, nor the fine artistic objects of the other two palaces, a fact which indicates the provincial character of this palace.

It is apparent from the advantageous position of the archaeological site that the town, whose ancient name remains unknown, was an important shipping and commercial centre for the Minoans. Excavations were begun in 1915 by Joseph Hadjidakis and are being continued by the French School of Archaeology.

In the Minoan town, apart from the palace, several private houses and the Chrysolakkos tombs have also been excavated.

The area had been inhabited since Neolithic times.

The first palace was built around 1900 BC, was destroyed around 1700 BC, following which a new one was built. However, around 1450 BC, this new palace suffered the same fate.

The ruins to be seen on the northwestern side, belong to the old palace, while the remainder of the ruins belong to the new palace.

The Palace

It is a two–storey edifice. The visitor enters it through the *western* paved court along the *processional way.* To the southeast there is a great *central court* in the middle of which are the four bases of an altar. The west wing of the palace to the west of the central court, includes several important rooms. The *loggia* is an open space with stairs leading to the court. At the end is a small staircase.

In a small room nearby, a jar was found that contained a sceptre with the figure of a panther and, outside the jar, were discovered a knife and a long sword (Herakleion Archaeological Museum). From the finds, it is conjectured that this area may possibly have been the place where the High Priest prepared himself for some sacred ritual, which was performed in the loggia, to which he had access through the stair case.

Futher to the south is an important area including a *crypt* and an *anteroom with a bench.* The two square columns of the crypt are inscribed with ritual symbols: a double axe, a trident, a star. It appears that this area was reserved for sacred ceremonies.

To the southwest of the court there are wide steps which may have been *the-atre seats.* Nearby is the *kernos,* a stone

vessel in which offerings were deposited, and which had a large central cavity with smaller ones around it.

In the southwestern corner of the central court, beside the *paved entrance,* there are two adjoining areas which served as *sanctuaries* for the south wing. Here was found a stone altar with carved symbols, earthen pots, an incense burner and other ritual objects.

At the western end of the area are the so-called *granaries* which had a vaulted roof supported by a central pillar.

Almost the entire *eastern wing* of the palace was taken up by *storerooms,* as we can see from the jars which were found here. These rooms are ranged in a parallel line and perpendicularly to the long *corridor of the storerooms,* which runs almost the entire length of the eastern wing, behind an elongated colonnade.

The northern side of the court is surrounded by colums joined together by a wall. Behind these is the *pillared hall.*

To the northwest of this room, the structure placed at an angle was a *Mycenean sanctuary.*

To the west of the pillared hall, next to a *paved corridor,* is the *Tower court.* Further to the west an area, the *polythyron,* is believed to have been the *royal residence* and to the south, adjoining the royal residence, there is an *area for ritual ceremonies,* with a square column; here pots, clay tablets, disks and staffs with hieroglyphic inscriptions were found.

To the north of the Tower court is the *northern court* of the palace which is surrounded by *workshops* and *storerooms.*

Here was the northern entrance, from which a paved road led to the sea.

Minoan residential quarters

Around the palace various residential quarters had developed, which made up the Minoan town. A number of houses have been excavated. One of the houses in the wealthy neighbourhood to the northwest of the palace has been restored and today houses a variety of finds.

The Minoan harbour and cemetery

The road leads from the northern gate of the palace to the site known today as Aghia Varvara, where there is a small bay, used by the Minoans as a port.

Here Minoan potsherds and tombs were excavated.

At a distance of 500 m., approximately, to the north of the palace, in the area today called *Chrysolakkos,* excavations begun in 1921 and continued for a long time, brought to light a square structure containing burial chambers. The area was used as a Minoan cemetery, but also as a sacred area for the worship of the dead.

Here, among other precious finds, was brought to light a part of the magnificent gold necklace, the pendant with the bees, which graces the Herakleion Archaeological Museum. It is an extremely elegant and fine example of Minoan metalwork, made with great skill and attention to detail.

At the 38.5 km. to the right is the beginning of the new national road towards Aghios Nikolaos. However, we shall continue our journey along the old na-

The coastal settlement of Sisi.

tional road. At the 41st km. to the left, we come to a crossroad leading to the seaside settlement of *Sisi,* in a sandy bay.

At the 42nd km. is the picturesque chapel of *Saint George of Selinari,* on the left side of a lovely gorge and, further on, the village of *Vrahassi.*

At the 48.5 km., a detour to the north leads to *Milato* and then to *Milato beach,* on the Cretan Sea. Near the village, on the side of a steep ravine, is the *Milato Cave* (20 mins. on foot), with a rich decor of stalactites and stalagmites. Inside the cave, which is approximately 300 m. long, a small chapel has been built and dedicated to Saint Thomas, and here, each year, during the service on the Saint's day, a prayer is said for the Cretans who were massacred on this spot by the Turks in 1823.

At *Latsida* (50.5 kms. from Herakleion) there are the churches of Panaghia (the Holy Virgin) and Aghia Paraskevi, both with frescoes.

Continuing to the southeast from Latsida we come to *Neapolis* (52.5 kms. from Herakleion).

Neapolis is situated in the heart of a fertile valley, called "the trough of Merabello". It was the capital of the Lasithi prefecture until 1904, when Aghios Ni-

kolaos took over the title. It has an *archaeological collection* with finds from the excavations at Elounda, Aghios Nikolaos and Dreros, as well as a *Folk Art museum* exhibiting various traditional objects, utensils, items of furniture and other hand–made articles.

The imposing church of the village, Megali Panaghiá, celebrates its feast day on August 15th. From Neapolis a road to the northwest leads to the Lasithi plateau.

To the northeast of Neapolis, on the hill of Aghios Antonios, is the site of *ancient Dreros,* where an oblong structure has been excavated, which is believed to have been a shrine dedicated to Apollo. Here, three bronze statues of the 7th century BC. (now in the Archaeological Museum of Herakleion), as well as inscriptions carved on a square stone in the Doric dialect, were found by villagers from the area.

After Neapolis we come to the village of Nikithianos and, a few kilometres further to the south, another branch of the road leads to the Lasithi plateau (see route 3).

We continue south and arrive at the end of our journey, at *Aghios Nikolaos* (68 kms. from Herakleion).

Herakleion – tour of the Lasithi plateau – visit of the Dicte cave

Herakleion – Kato Gouves – Potamiés – Sfendyli – Avdou – Goniés – Kerá – Vidianí – Psychró – Dicte cave – Kroustallenia Monastery – Tzermiado – Lagou – Vidiani – Krássi – Mochós – Stalis.

We follow the Herakleion – Aghios Nikolaos road up to the 23rd km., where the road to the south leads to *Potamiés* (34 km. from Herakleion). Near the village is the old monastery of Panaghia Gouverniotissa, of which the only part still standing is the church of the Panaghia, dedicated to the Dormition of the Virgin, and in which can be seen frescoes of the 14th century. We continue to the southeast towards Sfendyli, Avdou, Goniés (40.5 km.).

Forty–three kilometres from Herakleion, a road to the left leads towards Mochos and then joins the national road from Herakleion to Aghios Nikolaos (see route 2). Further along the road to the south are the settlements of *Krássi* and *Kerá*.

Near the neighbourhoods of Ano and Kato Kerá and in a superb setting with a beautiful view is the *monastery of Panaghia Kardiotissa* or *Kerá* (Lady), dedicated to the Birthday of the Holy Virgin, which is commemorated on September 8th. The church incorporates four buildings, the oldest of which is adorned with 14th century frescoes. In the monastery is kept an icon of the "Virgin Enchained", believed to be miraculous.

We continue to the south. At the 54th km., at the village of *Pikianó*, near which there is a lovely monastery dedicated to the Life–Giving Fountain (Zoödochos Pighi) of Vidiani, the road forks out, to the right and to the left, encircling the *Lasithi plateau*.

We take the left fork, traversing the plateau from right to left.

The view from high up on the road is magnificent. The picturesque windmills work regularly to water the fertile plain which covers an area of approximately 25,000 sq. km.

As the excavations carried out on various sites have shown, this inaccessible area, encircled by high mountain ranges, has been inhabited since Neolithic times.

During the period of Venetian rule and later under the Turkish occupation, the region was at the forefront of the resistance movement, with various uprisings starting from it. It was also a place of refuge for those who were being hunted by the occupiers.

As we continue our circle and pass through the villages of Kato Metochi, Aghios Charalambos, Plati, we come to *Psychró*, 63.5 kms. from Herakleion, situated at an altitude of 840 m. From here a road of one kilometre in length leads to a tourist pavillion and parking lot. If we take a footpath for about another kilometre, we arrive at the entrance of the *Dicte Cave*, at an altitude of 1025 metres above sea level.

Many mythological tales are associated with this dark, mysterious cave. From the archaeological finds, it has been established that this was a place of worship from Middle Minoan to Archaic times. An altar was discovered, tables for libations, numerous offerings, figurines, weapons, double axes, clay pots, rings, seals, precious stones etc.

The entrance is through an enormous

opening which lights up the deepest recesses of the cave, which consists of a large chamber. This large chamber is divided in its lower part into four smaller areas, all of which are adorned with stalactites and stalagmites. In the southern part there is a small lake.

From Psychro the road leads east, towards Kaminaki, Aghios Georgios and the *Kroustallenia monastery* (72 kms.) which is built on the eastern side of the plateau, on an imposing wooded hill. It is dedicated to the Dormition of the Virgin.

The monastery, as is the case with others in Crete, played an important role, during the Turkish occupation, as a centre of the revolutionary committee and as a school for the Greek children of the region.

Bronze statuette from the Dictaean Cave (Archaeological Museum of Herakleion).

The Dictaean Cave: the Lake.

Beyond the monastery, the road forks out again. The part that continues to the northeast ends, after a tiring but lovely drive, at Neapolis, going through the villages of Mesa Lasithi, Mesa Potami, Exo Potami, Zenia and Vrysses.

The other fork continues to the northwest, completing the circle. In this last part we meet the village of *Tzermiado* (74.5 kms.) which is the largest village of the plateau.

In excavated sites near the village were found Neolithic graves and Minoan structures. In particular, on the peak of Karfi, to the north of the village, a Minoan settlement was uncovered. Among its findings was the statue of a goddess, about a metre in height, which is now in the Herakleion Archaeological Museum.

To the east of Tzermiado is the *Trapeza Cave,* also known as the *Cronion* cave. This cave was used successively as a habitation, a burial area and an area of worship.

Sir Arthur Evans found here a faience statuette and gold leaves. Here were also discovered figurines made of ivory, wearing the "vraka" or aprons. In its low entrance were scattered various objects, mostly of a ritual character, dating from the Neolithic, early Minoan, Middle Minoan, Hellenistic and Byzantine periods.

We continue towards Lagou and Pikiano (77 kms.), from where we return by the same road in a northerly direction until we arrive at the intersection leading towards Goniés (43 km.). We continue towards Mochos and the main Herakleion – Aghios Nikolaos road, joining the road at its 31.5 km. mark (see route 2).

4

Herakleion – Karteros junction – cave of Eileithyia – Angarathos monastery – (Sambas – Apostoloi) – Kastelli – Lyttos – Thrapsano – Myrtia or Varvaroi – Houdetsi – Epanosifi monastery.
Return: Vathypetro – Archanes – Knossos – Herakleion.

From the Karteros junction, after the 8th km. from Herakleion, a right detour in the road leads to the cave of *Eileithyia*. According to mythology, this is where Hera gave birth to Eileithyia, the goddess of childbirth. The cave is mentioned by Homer and Strabo. The excavations here were begun by Joseph Hadjidakis and were continued by Spyros Marinatos.

The cave is long and narrow (length 64.5 m., width 9–12 m.) and measures 3–4.5 m. in height.

The entrance is through an opening on the east side. Approximately in the centre of the cave, a rectangular wall surrounds two cylindrical stalagmites which resemble figures of a mother and child.

It is believed that these stalagmites were objects of worship. From the finds, which include a kind of altar and a number of potsherds scattered about, archaeologists concluded that the cave had been a place of worship since Neolithic times and up to the 5th century AD.

The Cave of Eileithyia. These stalagmites resemble the figures of a mother and child.
Above: Archanes. The cemetery at Phourni.

Further along the road to the south and passing through the villages of Stamnoi, Episkopi, Sgourokephali, we come to the *Angarathos monastery* (23 kms. from Herakleion), an important monastery dedicated to the Dormition of the Virgin. It owes its name to the "angarathiá" (a type of bush) under which the icon of the Virgin was found. The church was later built on this spot. It is one of the oldest monasteries in Crete and is mentioned in documents of the 16th century.

It played an important part in the defense of the island against the Turks, when the latter made their attempts to take Crete from the Venetians.

In the village of *Sambas* there is a fork to the east leading to the villages of Apostoloi and *Kastelli* Pediadas (36 kms. from Herakleion). Kastelli is an attractive small town which owes its name to a Venetian castle which no longer exists. At the entrance of the town was found a Roman cemetery. Further to the east, beyond the village of Xidias, lie the ruins of ancient *Lyttos* or *Lyktos,* a strong town which was a rival of Knossos. Systematic excavations have not been carried out in this area. Lyttos was built on a naturally fortified site, at the foot of Mount Dicte — to which is owes its surname of Dictaea — and, for this reason, was not walled.

Archanes.

Although it was a very ancient city —
as has been established – it attained its
acme in historic times. In 220 BC it was
destroyed by its rival, Knossos, with the
help of the powerful city of Gortyn.

As an autonomous city, Lyttos minted
its own coins and, during Roman times,
it acquired great fame. It had an aqueduct, an acropolis, a theatre and statues of Roman emperors adorning various sites. Today these statues are kept
in the Archaeological Museum of Herakleion.

We return to Kastelli and, approximately one kilometre further on, we
turn left and, driving southwestwards,
we pass through *Thrapsanó,* the village
of the potters, as it was called by the
Turks, since most of its inhabitants
were potters and created jars for storing agricultural products.

To the east of the village is the church of
Kato Panaghia or Panaghia Pigadiotis-
sa.

The road continues towards the northwest. We take the right fork before the
village of Aghies Paraskiés, to stop for a
while at *Myrtiá* or *Várvaroi.* Here, on
the village square, in a recently restored house owned by the Kazantzakis and
Anemoyiannis families, is housed the
Nikos Kazantzakis Museum, where
one can see personal objects and manuscripts belonging to the writer, all the
editions of his works, stage scenery and
costumes from performances of representative plays and an informative au-
dio–visual programme. (For information: tel. 081/742.451 and 741.689).

(Shorter route to the village of Myrtiá
from Herakleion through Knossos and
Skalani).

We descend, in a southwesterly direction, towards Aghies Paraskies, Aghios
Vassilios and Houdetsi. Five hundred
metres beyond Houdetsi the road towards the north leads to Vathypetros
and Epano Archanes. We follow the
road to the south and after 5.5 kms. a
road to the right (3 kms.) brings us to
the Aghios Georgios Apanosiphi mona-

stery. It is believed to have been built
around 1600 and it amassed a great
amount of wealth from the donations of
Venetian feudal lords.

During the Turkish occupation it was
an important cultural centre where
many churchmen were educated; at the
same time it was a refuge for Cretan
freedom fighters.

The monastery was destroyed twice
and rebuilt in the form it has today, in
1864. The church has two naves, the
right nave being dedicated to Saint
George and the left to the Transfiguration of the Lord. Today, in the monastery are kept many precious relics:
sumptuously bound copies of the New
Testament, chalices, ciboria, crosses,
sacerdotal vestments etc.

As we take the road back again and before we reach Houdetsi, we turn left for
Vathypetro and *Archanes.*

(N.B. The road between Houdetsi and
Vathypetro is a dirt road.) From there
we continue northwards towards Patsi-
des, Knossos, Herakleion.

(For a shorter road to Archanes, 15
kms, and Vathypetro – 20 kms. – take
the Herakleion – Knossos road. See
route 2).

At Piso Livadia, on the southeastern
flank of the Juktas mountain, the Minoan palace of Vathypetro was found
(excavated in 1949 by Professor Spyros
Marinatos).

Visit of Vathypetro

The Palace is a large building, parts of which are two storeys high, The walls are covered with polychrome plaster and there are no paintings. It is believed to have been built around 1600 BC, to have been destroyed and abandoned around 1500 BC while, later, its south side was repaired.

In the palace were found and restored an olive press and a wine press, finds which led archaeologists to the conclusion that this must have been a farmhouse. Weaving implements and potters' wheels were also discovered here.

The palace has a central court, a pillared room with four square columns, a storeroom containing sixteen jars and a sanctuary. One of the most important moveable finds was a large decorated amphora for carrying oil.

Three kilometres away, to the north of Vathypetro, is the lovely little town of *Epano Archanes,* situated in a fertile and well irrigated region, amid luxuriant vegetation and many vineyards. The town is reputed for its excellent wine and its raisins. This is where the ancient town of Acharna was situated.

Two and a half kilometres further north is the community of *Kato Archanes.*

Ancient Acharna was an important Minoan town which flourished between 2500 and 1400 BC. The excavations which were begun in 1964 by the archaeologists Yiannis and Effie Sakellaraki, are still being carried on today.

The areas that have been excavated are: part of a Minoan palace, a cemetery at Fourni and a Minoan temple at the site of Anemospiliá.

In this area, the archaeologists Spyros Marinatos and N. Platon also located a building of the early Hellenic period, as well as other buildings dating from Greco–Roman times.

Visit of Archanes

The Minoan palace

It lies in the old Turkish quarter, near the church of Panaghia, and is believed to have been destroyed in 1450 BC, at the same time as the other Minoan palaces.

Ruins of buildings around its northern entrance have been uncovered, as has a section of the eastern wing.

The Minoan cemetery

It lies on Fourni hill (1.5 kms. to the southwest of Pano Archarnes) and is considered the most important and most extensive prehistoric cemetery in the Aegean.

It was used between 2500 and 1250 BC, approximately. The funeral gifts which were found here are extremely rich and valuable and most of them are kept in the Herakleion Archaeological Museum. They include several small objects in gold, bronze and ivory, masterpieces of design and workmanship, which were found in a sarcophagus. It was the first royal tomb in Crete to have been found intact. In other tombs were found gold and silver jewellery, finely worked seals, figurines, pots etc.

The Minoan temple at Anemospylia

(5 kms, southwest of Archanes). This is a sanctuary in three sections with a long corridor built, as was the palace, of hewn stone, and surrounded by an enclosed courtyard. It was probably destroyed by an earthquake, at the same time as the Minoan palaces of Crete, in 1700 BC.

In the sanctuary were found ritual utensils, an offering table, an altar, a large stone basin, jars, two life–size clay feet, probably belonging to some statue that was an object of worship. The most important and most discussed find of the sanctuary, however, was the four human skeletons, one of which had a bronze sword on its breast, which led archaeologists to conjecture that these had been victims of ritual sacrifice.

Clay model of a house from Archanes (Archaeological Museum of Herakleion).

109

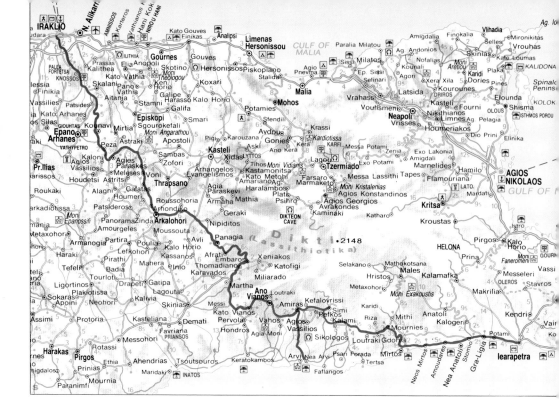

5

HERAKLEION – IERAPETRA

Herakleion – Knossos – Kounavi – Peza – Aghies Paraskies intersection – Arkalochori – Afrati – Ano Viannos Amiras – Arvi – Symi – Myrtos – Ierapetra.

We follow the road which leads from Herakleion to Knossos. To the south (15th km.) we meet the village of Kounavi, where capitals of Doric columns were found and also small clay votive tablets of the Hellenistic and Roman periods.

In the village there is a Byzantine church which is worth seeing. It has three naves and is dedicated to Christ the Lord, Saint Nicholas and Saint Demetrius. This church was decorated with frescoes, but these have not survived.

We continue southwards and, passing through the villages of Peza, Aghies Paraskiés (intersection), Melesses, Alagni, Houmeri, we come to Arkalochori (33 kms. from Herakleion), an important commercial centre. Six kilometres further along we come to a crossing; the road to the left leads to Mylos Gazepi and from there to Kastelli (10 kms from the intersection).

Just outside Arkalochori stands the Byzantine church of the Archangel Mi-

chael, with a painted inscription above one of its doors and important frescoes.

In 1932, on the Profitis Ilias hill, not far from the village, Spyros Marinatos and N. Platon discovered a Minoan sanctuary in a cave, which served as a place of worship from 2500 to 1450 BC, at which time it appears to have been destroyed. Among its rich finds, especially important are the double axes in gold, bronze and silver.

Some of these are decorated, and one of the bronze ones has an inscription in hieroglyphics, similar to those on the Phaestos disc (Herakleion Archaeological Museum). Another has an inscription in Linear A script. A number of daggers, swords (one of which is 1.055 m. in length), pots, etc. were also found her.

It is believed that a warrior deity must have been worshipped in the cave, which is why the offerings were mostly weapons.

Left: Ierapetra.
Above: Symi. The sacred mountain.
Hermes and Aphrodite.

Further south, after passing the village of Panaghia, on a detour to the right, we find the village of *Afrati*, near which were discovered a sanctuary, houses and vaulted tombs of the Geometric and Archaic periods, as well as a Hellenistic acropolis.

Further along the main road is the village of *Embaros*, with a church adorned with frescoes (Aghios Georgios).

Five kilometres further along from Embaros, we meet the village of *Martha* (54 kms. from Herakleion), from where a new road leads westwards towards Pyrgos and thence to the village of *Aghioi Deka* (see route 6).

From Martha the road continues southwards and after 5.5 kms. a right fork leads to the *bay of Keratókambos*.

Further along on the main road we come upon the village of Kato Viannos and *Ano Viannos* (65 kms. from Herakleion), the latter a verdant and amphitheatrically built village of some importance, at the foot of Mount Dicte, on the site of ancient Viannos. During the Turkish occupation and, also, in later years, during the German occupation, its inhabitants paid a heavy toll in blood for their resistance to the invaders. The churches of Aghia Pelagia (1360) and Aghios Georgios (1400), decorated with frescoes, are worth a visit. Outside the village two large tombs were discovered in the hollow of rocks, containing 30 burial pithoi.

Also on a height, in the same area, a house of the Middle Minoan period was found and, close by, a large Late Minoan settlement and a Middle Minoan house–sanctuary.

To the southeast, at the Amira – Arvi intersection, a monument has been erected to the inhabitants of the area who were executed by the occupying forces on September 14th, 1943.

A detour to the right brings us to *Arvi*. This is a lovely seaside village on the Libyan sea, with rich fruit orchards.

We return to Amira and continue eastwards.

After the villages of Kefalovryssi and Pefkos, a road leads to *Symi*, near which was found an important sanctuary dedicated to the god Hermes and to the goddess Aphrodite. The finds from the sanctuary are exhibited in the Herakleion Archaeological Museum.

The road continues eastwards towards *Gdochia*, Kalami, Loutraki, Mourniés and ends up at *Myrtos* on the Libyan sea.

From there it continues along the coast towards Neos Myrtos, Amoudares, Nea Anatoli, Stomio, Gra–Lygia, Potamoi and Ierapetra (106 kms. from Herakleion). All along the coast there are large greenhouses producing a rich crop of early fruit and vegetables.

East of Myrtos (3.5 km away) on a low hill known as *Fournou Korfi*, was found the prehistoric settlement of Myrtos, dating from the Early Minoan period.

Approximately 90 rooms and other areas, designed for a variety of uses, have been excavated. One of the rooms served as a sanctuary; here, the statue of a goddess was found. Also, among the ruins of the settlement were found a number of pots of excellent quality, stone seals, daggers, weaving implements and other objects, which today are exhibited in the Archaeological Museum of Aghios Nikolaos.

On another hill called *Pyrgos*, a second Minoan settlement was found, with an impressive two–storey or three–storey house on the top of the hill, belonging to the Neopalatial period. The house was destroyed around 1450 BC. Among the finds of Pyrgos are various ceramic libation cups and other elaborately worked pots.

Ierapetra

(106 kms. from Herakleion or 101 kms. through Aghios Nikolaos).

The abundant production of early fruit and vegetables grown in the greenhouses of the region, and the lovely beaches to the east and west of the town, have contributed to Ierapetra's becoming an important commercial and tourist centre in recent years.

Ierapetra - the beach and the modern town.

Ierapetra - the "Kalés".

It is a lively modern town with few remains of the past. On the site of the Ierapetra of today stood the important ancient city of Ierapytna, whose period of prosperity coincided with historic times. It was in constant conflict with Praessos, the very powerful town of eastern Crete, which did not allow Ierapytna to extend her territories.

Finally, in the 2nd century BC, Ierapytna prevailed over Praessos and subjugated the town and, with it, all its territories in the region. Thus its dominion extended over the entire southeastern coast and its period of prosperity lasted for many years. After fierce resistance, Ierapytna fell to the Romans in 66 BC, but continued to be a city of considerable importance even during Roman times, as is indicated by its coins and the important Roman finds unearthed here. It had impressive buildings, theatres, an aqueduct, public baths — none of these survive today — and was adorned with a great number of colossal statues. During the Byzantine period it still retained its importance. In 828, however, it was destroyed by the Saracens and its decay became final during the Venetian period. In 1647 it came under Turkish occupation.

In its harbour there are ruins of a Venetian castle (Kalés) which was rearranged by the Turks to fit their own needs, when they took the town.

In the old town there still stands a mosque and opposite this a beautiful restored fountain. The following churches are worthy of mention: Panaghitsa or Pangahia tou Kalé, the church of the Transfiguration of Christ, also called church of Christ the Lord, or just "The Saviour", Aghios Nikolaos, Aghios Ioannis, and the cathedral of Saint George, the town's patron saint, built in 1856.

In the *Ierapetra Archaeological Collection,* which is housed in the Ottoman School (Dimarcheion square, tel. 0842/22.246), are exhibited various objects found in the area and belonging to various periods. Among the most important are: ritual pots and other vessels, jars, axes, a clay potter's wheel, decorated sarcophagi, the Episkopi sarcophagus with twelve scenes depicted on it, figurines, red–figure pots, Roman lamps with decorations in relief, Greco–Roman statues found at Viglia and the statue of the goddess Demeter.

*Ierapetra, a commercial and tourist centre
in south-east Crete.*

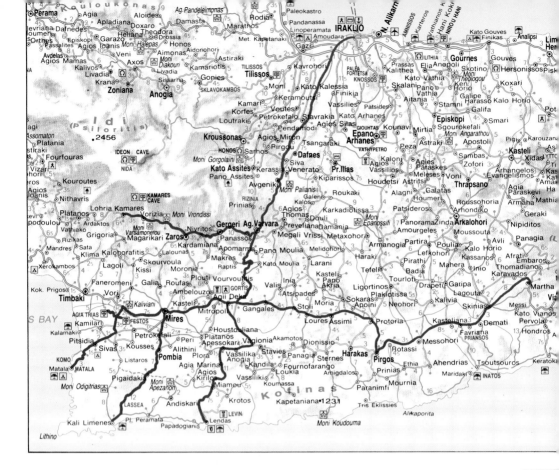

6

Herakleion – Paliani Monastery – Aghia Varvara (Vrontissi Monasstery – Varsamonero Monastery – Kamares) – Aghioi Deka (Gagales – Assimi – Martha), (Miamou, Lentas – Lebena) – Gortyna – Moires (Kaloi Limenes) – Phaestos – Aghia Triada – Matala.

We follow the road which leads from the Chania Gate towards the southwest, towards Aghia Varvara and Moires, passing through thickly planted vineyards.

At *Xenerato* (20 kms. from Herakleion) there is a detour to the left which leads to the old *convent of Paliani,* one of the most ancient monasteries of the island, as is indicated by its name (from "palaia"=old). Established in the first Byzantine period, we find it mentioned, since 668 AD, under names such as Pala and Palaia. The monastery was twice destroyed by the Turks.

The church has three naves, of which the central nave is dedicated to the Dormition of the Virgin (celebrated on the 15th of August), while the other two are dedicated to the three great Fathers of the Church: Basil the Great, Gregory the Theologian and John Chrysostom, and to Saint Panteleimon, respectively. From the main road we continue southwards, passing through *Aghia Varvara* (29.5 kms. from Herakleion). Here we find the chapel of Profitis Elias which, according to local tradition, marks the geographical centre of Crete. To the

View of the archaeological site of Phaestos.
Above: Propalatial Kamares style vase, from Phaistos.

northwest of Aghia Varvara, on the hill called "Patella tou Prinia", lie the ruins of *ancient Rizinia,* which was excavated by the Italian School of Archaeology.

A detour from Aghia Varvara to the west leads to Zaro, to the monasteries of Vrontissi and Aghios Fanourios of Varsamonero, and to Kamares, going through charming villages set amid lush vegetation, through which flow streams of crystal water. On the southerly foothills of the Psiloritis mountain, with a magnificent view towards the *plain of Messará,* stands the Vrontissi monastery.

Its church has two naves, one of which is dedicated to St. Anthony, the other to St. Thomas.

The monastery may have got its name from its owner, as was often the case with other monasteries on Crete, but we do not know exactly when it was founded — certainly before 1400, a date mentioned in manuscripts.

During the Venetian period, it was an important cultural centre where the arts and letters flourished, while during the Turkish occupation the monastery played an important role in the struggle against the occupiers. A few 14th century frescoes still survive.

The church belfry is very characteristic and one of the oldest on Crete. It is covered by arches and stands at some distance from the church. At the entrance there is a most elegant Venetian fountain of the 15th century with a depiction in the centre, in relief, of God and Adam and Eve in Paradise, and with four figures at the lower edge which symbolize the rivers of Eden and from whose mouths water flows.

Further along the road to the west, we come to the village of *Voriza,* and the *monastery of Varsamónero.* Today, only the church still stands, with its three naves, dedicated to the Virgin Mary, to St. John the Forerunner and to Saint Fanourios. It has a rich decoration of frescoes which are very important in Cretan hagiography. Apart from the frescoes there are also some very precious icons, a beautiful wood–carved iconostasis and an important inscription with the date of the rebuilding of the church. The woodcarved episcopal throne and lectern, which are exhibited in the Historical Museum of Herakleion, both belong to the Varsamonero monastery.

Further to the west lies the village of *Kamáres* (26.5 kms. from Aghia Varvara), at an altitude of 600 m. To the northeast of the village, on a ridge of the Psiloritis mountain (altitude 1525 m.) is the *Cave of Kamáres.*

This cave can only be reached on foot (4–5 hours' walk). It is known for the famous Kamares pots of 2000 BC which were found here, and which were used by the faithful for libations. The cave, which was discovered by accident in 1890, by a villager, was explored shortly afterwards by Italian archaeologists and, in 1913, by the British School of Archaeology.

It is believed that, in Neolithic times, it was used as a dwelling place while, in Minoan times, it was a place of worship.

Continuing on our main route from Aghia Varvara and, passing through the fertile plain of Messara, we come to *Aghioi Deka,* a village which owes its name to the ten early Christian Martyrs who were beheaded at a short di-

Gortys.
Above: The temple of Apollo.
Below: Partial view.

stance from the spot where, later, a Byzantine church was built in their honour and named after them. (Aghioi Deka intersection, 44 kms. from Herakleion).

Just before entering the village, a road leads eastwards towards Gagales, Assimi, Praetoria, Pyrgos, Kastellianá, ending up at the village of *Martha* (see route 5).

Between Aghioi Deka and the Metropolis lie the ruins of ancient *Gortys.*

Visit of Gortys.

Gortys, or Gortyna, as it is called today, was one of the strongest and most ancient towns of Crete and, during Roman and early Byzantine times, the capital of the island. In the 3rd century BC it captured Phaestos and its port, Matala, and thus had two ports: Lebena and Matala. It was in constant conflict with Knossos, but cultivated peaceful relations with the Achaeans and the Ptolemies of Egypt. During the period of Roman domination it knew its greatest period of prosperity, since it took the side of the Romans and did not put up a resistance against them. In exchange, not only did the Romans not destroy the city, as they had done the other towns which had resisted, but they also helped it extend its domination over the island, and established it as the seat of the Roman praetorians.

Gortyna accepted Christianity early and became the see of the first Bishop of Crete, the Apostle Titus. In the early Byzantine period it flourished and retained its prestige until 828 AD, when it was taken and destroyed by the Saracens.

From that time on, the town was deserted and was never again inhabited.

The most interesting monuments of the Gortyna archaeological site are:

On the right bank of the Lethaean torrent, on a height, the remains of an *acropolis* and to its southeast, the *seats of an ancient theatre.* On the other bank can be seen the *Odeon,* which was

119

The famous Codes of Law of Gortys.

built on the site of an older square structure during the 1st century AD.

For its reconstruction, the stones of a nearby archaic circular building were used, on which were carved the famous *laws of Gortys.* On the northwestern side of the Odeon, four rows of the precious inscribed stones still survive today, constituting the most important record of the Law of the time and an invaluable aid for the study of its inscriptions.

The inscriptions are carved in the Doric dialect, "boustrophedon", that is, "as the ox plows", (from left to right and then right to left and so on) and they date from the end of the 6th century BC. Nearby, there stood the *agora* with the *sanctuary of Asclepios,* where the statue of Asclepiades was found (Herakleion Archaeological Museum) and, further to the south, the ruins of the *basilica of St. Titus,* an impressive church built with massive carved limestone blocks. The portion which survives is covered by an arch.

Architectural elements from the church and precious religious vessels are kept in the Historical Museum of Herakleion.

On the Gortyna site there are also re-

mains of the *Roman Praetorium* (a building of the 4th century AD), of two *Nymphaea* (shrines dedicated to the Nymphs), of a *sanctuary* dedicated to the *Pythian Apollo,* of the *sanctuary of the Egyptian deities,* of *two theatres,* an *amphitheatre,* an *aqueduct,* and *warm baths.*

In the *Gortyna museum* are exhibited finds discovered on the site.

Continuing from Aghioi Deka to Moires and just outside Aghioi, the road forks out. The left fork, with a southerly direction, passes through the villages of Metropolis, Houstoulianá, Platanos, Plora, Apesokari, Aghia Marina, Miamou, and ends up at *Lentas,* a seaside settlement on the south coast with a lovely beach and a limpid sea.

At the villages of Platanos, Plora and Apesokari, early Minoan graves have been excavated.

To the east of Lentas, lies the ancient port of Gortyna, *Lebena.* The excavations of the area brough to light ruins of the Greco–Roman period which coincides with the time when the town and port were at the height of their prosperity. The most important of these ruins are: the sanctuary of Asclepios, a fountain, the Avaton (the "untrodden"

– the inner sanctum), a gallery, fonts where patients used to bathe, two hostels for visitors, the remains of an ancient bridge.

To the east of the site, on the ruins of a Byzantine 9th century basilica, stands the small chapel of St. John (14th or 15th century) with vestiges of frescoes. In the same area were found vaulted graves of the early Minoan period.

We continue on our main route towards the west and, after 8.5 kilometres from Aghioi Deka, we come to the modern town of *Moires* (53 kms. from Herakleion), a road junction and an important commercial centre for the area.

From here there is a road south towards Pombia, Pigaidakia and *Kaloi Limenes.* It is said that it was in this picturesque settlement of Kaloi Limenes that the Apostle Paul landed, when he was being taken to Rome. To the east and west there are lovely beaches and, opposite them, the islets of *Megalo* and *Mikro Nissi.* To the east there lies *Ancient Lassaea,* where early Minoan vaulted graves and ruins of the Roman period have been found. On the main route, going west towards Tymbaki and at a distance of 7.5 kms. from Moires,

we turn left and, after two kilometres, we come to *Phaestos,* 63 kms, from Herakleion.

Visit of Phaestos

Second in importance only to Knossos, from the archaeological point of view, is *Phaestos.* It lies 62.5 kms. southwest of Herakleion, to which it is linked through regurlar services by KTEL bus. It is built on a hill (at an altitude of 100 m., approximately, above sea level), south of the Lythaeon river, and commands the fertile plain of Kato Messara, which is surrounded by impressive mountains (Psiloritis, Asteroussia, the Lasithi mountains, far away in the background). To the south lies the Libyan sea. Phaestos, owing to its importance, is mentioned in the texts of ancient writers (Diodorus, Strabo, Pausanias), but also by Homer.

According to mythology, the dynasty which ruled Phaestos was that of Rhadamanthys, son of Zeus and brother of Minos.

Palace of Phaestos. Propylaea and part of the West Court.

PHAESTOS - PLAN OF THE PALACE

1. WEST COURT
2. PROCESSIONAL WAY
3. PROPYLON OF THE OLD PALACE
4. THEATRE
5. SANCTUARY
6. PROPYLAEA STAIRWAY OF THE NEW PALACE
7. WEST PROPYLON
8. STOREROOMS
9. CORRIDOR
10. LUSTRAL BASIN OF THE OLD PALACE
11. PRIESTS' ROOMS
12. TEMPLE OF RHEA
13. CENTRAL COURT
14. LUSTRAL BASIN
15. EAST PORTICO
16. ENTRANCE TO NORTH WING
17. NORTH COURT
18. EAST COURT
19. WORKSHOPS
20. QUEEN'S ROOM
21. KING'S MEGARON
22. SITE WHERE THE DISC OF PHAESTOS WAS DISCOVERED
23. POTTERS' WORKSHOP

It was a very strong, rich, populous and independent city. It minted its own coins and, at the acme of its power and prosperity, its domination extended from the Lithino point to the Melissa point and included the islets of Paximadia (Letoae was their ancient name). The state of Phaestos also disposed of two strong ports, Matala and Kommos to the southwest.

The area had been inhabited since Neolithic times (3000 BC approximately), as is evidenced by the foundations of Neolithic habitations, the tools, figurines and potsherds which were discovered under the storerooms of the palace, during the excavations which were carried out there.

The first palace was built in approximately 1900 BC and, together with the other structures around, covered an area of 18,000 sq.m (slightly less than that of the palace of Knossos). The great earthquake which occurred a-

round 1700 BC was the cause of its destruction, as it was of that of Knossos. In its place a new, more impressive palace was built, to which belong the greater part of the ruins which have been restored, while several parts of the first palace have also been excavated, mainly those lying to the southwest.

After the discovery of the southern part of the palace, during the excavations by D. Levi, various converging clues which came to light, seemed to lead to the conclusion that the second palace, too, was destroyed by an earthquake, when the southern part of the hill subsided and carried along with it the southern part of the palace and the central court.

Despite the recurring destruction of the palace, Phaestos continued to flourish during the Archaic, Classical and Hellenistic periods until, around 200 BC, it was destroyed by its rival, Gortys, with which it was in constant conflict. In spite of this, life continued in Phaestos during the Roman period as well.

The excavations of the area, begun in 1900 by the Italian School of Archaeology, under Federico Halbherr, were continued under L. Pernier and D. Levi and brought to light extremely important finds from the Minoan, Geometric and Hellenistic periods.

The Palace

The palace buildings of Phaestos were developed around a court called the *central court*. The main entrance was through the northwestern side, along a paved court, the *west court*. In this area there are ruins dating from historic times. A *processional way* crosses the court diagonally. At its northern end there is a series of eight tiers 22 m. in length, which were used as theatre seats and, at the end of the road to the south, we find the *propylon of the Old Palace* with a single column. At the northeastern end of the western court is a *sanctuary* consisting of four small connecting rooms with benches. These contained offering tables, pots and other vessels used for the sacrifice. Behind the sanctuary is the *propylaeon stairway* of the new palace and, after

Storerooms.

123

General view of Phaestos.

*Pithoi with decoratio
in relief, from
Phaestos.*

that, the *propylaeon.* To the southeast of the propylaea, next to the light well, a narrow stairway leads to the *antechamber of the storerooms* which communicates with a corridor, to the right and left of which were the *storerooms.* Next to the storerooms, to the right of the stairway, is the room of the *lustral basin,* a remnant of the old palace. A wide *corridor,* parallel to that of the storerooms, links the western court with the central court, a part of which, to the southeast, has subsided. The part of the palace which is situated in the middle of the western part of the central court consists of small *sanctuary rooms,* as is witnessed by votive objects which were discovered in them. In some, double axes, symbols of Minoan worship, were actually found inscribed on the walls.

At the southwestern end of the palace, outside the palace precincts, we can still see the ruins of the archaic *temple of Rhea.*

Along the eastern side of the central court extends the eastern wing of the palace. From its northern corner begins a narrow *corridor* leading eastwards, and separating the eastern and the northern wings. South of the corridor there are four connecting rooms: the first was a *polythyron,* the second served as a light well, the third was the anteroom and the fourth — further to the south in relation to the corridor — was a lustral area. Here rhytons were found, a pitcher, stone horns and double axes. It is believed that, after the palace was destroyed, during the time of the Achaean domination, this area was still used for religious ceremonies. A *portico* in the shape of a right an-

gle with a colonnade is found to the east of these rooms.

Access to the northern wing of the palace is through the centre of the north side of the central court, where the royal apartments are to be found.

At the *entrance* there were two half columns, of which the stone bases are still extant. From here an outdoor, *paved passage* begins. It has a conduit for draining off the rainwater, and ends up in the small *northern court*. To the right and left of the passage are small rooms. Another passage, to the east of the northern court, leads to a larger *eastern court*, in the centre of which is a sort of oven. This must have served as a furnace for melting metals or as a kiln for baking pots. On this spot were found, also, two clay potter's wheels. These finds led archaeologists to the conclusion that the row of rooms on the western side of the court must have been *workshops.*

From the northern court a *corridor* leading north brings us to the royal apartments, on a lower level. To the left of the corridor is found the *queen's chamber.*

Behind this room a narrow stairway led to the upper floor. To the north of the queen's chamber was the *king's residence,* adorned, as was the queen's, with sumptuous frescoes and paved with alabaster flagstones with red joints.

The northeastern portion of the palace constitutes an independent area which belongs to the Pre–palatial period and is connected functionally to the palace. In one of the rooms of this area was found the famous *Phaestos disc,* with the hieroglyphic script printed in a spiral form on both of its faces, while the clay was still damp. It is a unique monument of its kind and is exhibited in the archaeological museum of Herakleion.

At a distance of 2800 m. to the west of Phaestos, on a hill overlooking the fertile valley of Tymbaki, lie the ruins of the *small palace or royal villa of Aghia Triada.*

Visit of Aghia Triada

To the southwest of the archaeological site stands the 14th century church of Aghia Triada. From this church, which has two naves, the little mediaeval village which used to stand here before it was destroyed by the Turks in 1897, got its name. The Minoan name of the area is unknown to us.

The royal villa or small Minoan palace of Aghia Triada, as it was named by the Italian archaeologists who discovered it in the early years of our century, was built around 1600 BC, on a hill which had been inhabited since Neolithic times. It is believed that it served as a summer residence of the king of Phaestos, with which Aghia Triada was linked by a paved road. Around 1450 BC, it was destroyed, and on its ruins were built a new rectangular building and a portico. Later, the villa was no longer used as a residence, but served as a place of worship, as the rich religious objects found here testify.

The visit begins from the western side, where the small chapel of St. George now stands. This chapel has a single nave, a tiled roof, and dates from the 14th century.

A *polythyron* leads from approximately the centre of the *western wing* to a *portico* and a *light well* to the east.

Further on there is a *room with benches* and another smaller room with an alabaster platform, which may perhaps have served as a bed.

In the area to the northeast of the *polythyron* was found a *collection of clay seals* and, beyond that, a room with frescoes depicting lilies and wild cats (Archaeological Museum of Herakleion). In a nearby area were found nineteen copper talents (Archaelogical Museum of Herakleion) from which it was conjectured that the room was used as a *treasury.*

View of the archaeological site of Aghia Triada.

The *storerooms* were situated in the southern part of the western wing.

In the northern wing there is a store-room with a central square pier and, to the east, a *long and narrow hall* for the reception of important guests. Further to the east is the staircase. Behind it there is a *portico with five square columns.* To the northeast of the portico is the *rectangular agora of the Achaean period.*

On the eastern side of the agora stood a row of alternating square and round columns and, in front of these, were eight rooms — possibly *shops* — containing large clay jars.

To the west of the agora were found remains of Minoan houses.

The eastern wing consisted of the *servants quarters* and of a *consecrated area* with a bench. In the central court were found ruins of Achaean buildings and, in the southeastern part, the beginning of a paved way which led to Phaestos. At a distance of 150 m. to the northeast of the villa were found two beehive tombs with many burials and rich funeral offerings. To the south of these tombs were found a number of other single rectangular tombs. In one of these was discovered the well–known stone sarcophagus of Aghia Triada, decorated on all four of its sides with paintings and religious scenes (Archaeological Museum of Herakleion).

Continuing to the southwest and passing through Pitsidia, we end up at *Mátala* (75 kms. from Herakleion), the port of Phaestos and, during the Roman period, of Gortyna. To the right is the Bay of *Kommós,* the second port of Phaestos. The excavations which are still going on in the area have brought to light many interesting and important finds.

The Harvesters' jar from the excavations at Aghia Triada- the most important stone jar exhibited in the Archaeological Museum of Herakleion.

One side of the stone sarcophagus of Aghia Triada (Archaeological Museum of Herakleion)

Matala.

Mátala, only a small fishing village a few years ago, has now developed into a modern holiday centre providing hotel accommodation, rooms to rent and pensions for a good number of visitors.

There are also camping sites, restaurants, tavernas, and many shops.

The hollowed-out rocks with the artificial caves are the characteristic feature of the village. Some of these may possibly have been used as prehistoric dwellings while, during the 1st and 2nd centuries, they were used as tombs. Today the area is an archaeological site and has been fenced off.

The beach of Mátala opens like an embracing arm into the Libyan sea. Its golden sand, clear waters and the mysterious rocks attract many visitors to this corner of the island.

At the 3.5 km of the Phaestos – Mátala road, a fork to the left leads towards Siva, to the *Hodegetria monastery* and ends at Kaloi Limenes.

The *Hodegetria monastery* has several icons worth mentioning, as well as a collection of holy vestments. Its church has two naves, and is dedicated to the Birthday of the Holy Virgin and to the Holy Apostles. The monastery used to be surrounded by a wall, the north gate of which, inscribed with the date 1568, still stands.

In the area of the monastery was excavated a burial complex consisting of five chambers, two vaulted tombs and a paved court within a precinct. In the tombs were found clay and stone pots, gold jewellery, bronze tools and many seals.

Matala.
A beach with golden sand,
sparkling waters
and impressive
rock formations.

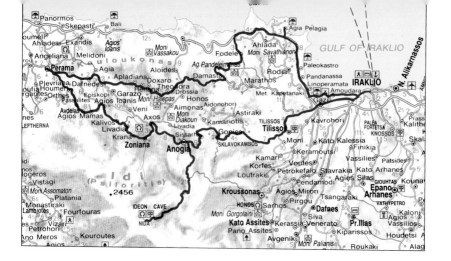

7

Herakleion – Gházi – Tylissós – Goniés – Idaean Cave – Anógheia – Axós – Zonianá – Pérama – Damásta – Fódele – exit towards new national road along the coast – Aghia Pelaghia – Palaeokastro – Linoperámata – Ammoudára – Herakleion.

We start off from Herakleion and head towards the west. Passing through the village of Ghazi, at the 10th km. we come to an intersection and, taking the left fork, we come to Tylissos (14 kms. west of Herakleion) in a valley planted whith vineyards and olive trees.

Visit of Tylissós

Tylissos, which retains its pre–Hellenic name, was one of the most important Minoan towns, as evidenced by the excavations there, which brought to light precious finds: clay pithoi, amphorae, pitchers, cooking utensils, incense burners, tablets inscribed in Linear A script, seals, stone vessels and implements, offertory tables, large copper cauldrons, double axes, wall–paintings, a bronze figurine of a man in an attitude of worship, and others (Archaeological Museum of Herakleion).

Unlike Knossos, Phaestos and Mallia, at Tylissos no palace was found; however, three large, separate structures, were characterized by J. Hadjidakis, who excavated the site, as "houses". They belong to the Late Minoan period and include, as do the palaces, outdoor courts, areas of worship, storerooms, stairways, servants' quarters, living areas, corridors, etc. A water supply network and a circular cistern were also found.

Left: Aghia Pelagia and Lygaria.
Above: Archaeological site of Tylisos.

As we continue towards the west, between Tylissos and Goniés, in a long and narrow valley called *"Sklavókambos"*, we come to the site of the ruins of the Minoan megaron (villa) of Sklavókambos, which dates from approximately 1500 BC.

Goniés (26 kms. from Herakleion) is a mountain village, built amphitheatrically on the flank of a mountain, with a magnificent view. Further on and just before we get to Anogheia, at the 36th km., a road to the left leads to the *Nida plateau,* to the Psiloritis Mountain and ends at the *Idaean cave,* after a drive of 21 kms. (for half of this distance the road is tarred, the remainder is a dirt road).

According to mythology, this is where Zeus was brought up, and a number of festivals in his honour were held in this cave.

It is considered certain that the Idaean cave served as a place of worship until Roman times.

It was discovered entirely by accident by a shepherd, in 1884, and was explored for the first time the following year. New excavations which were begun in 1982 by the archaeologist, G. Sakellarakis, have brought to light a number of finds, which testify to human presence in this cave from the end of the Neolithic period.

Among these are: iron weapons and implements, bronze vessels and figurines, bronze votive shields engraved with hunting scenes, bone and ivory objects etc. (Archaeological Museum of Herakleion).

*A daily scene
in the picturesque little streets of Anogheia.*

The cave is at an altitude of 1,540 m. above sea level, has an impressive entrance, a large chamber followed by two horizontal ones, while between these and perpendicularly to them opens up the "Adyton" (the "untrodden" – or inner sanctum).

As we continue our route, we come to *Anogheia* (36.5 kms.), built on the northern foothills of the Psiloritis Mountain, near the boundaries of the prefectures of Herakleion and Rethymnon.

It is a fairly large town renowned for its rich traditions, picturesque customs, meat and dairy products and genuine Cretan handwoven articles.

During the Turkish occupation, the people of Anogheia played an important role in the struggle for independence, as they did during the German occupation, when they organised a fierce resistance movement against the occupiers. German reprisals were not long in coming: the town was razed to the ground on August 15th, 1944, and many of its inhabitants were executed.

Today, Anogheia is an important centre of tourist activity and offers a good number of beds in small hotels and homes. There are also restaurants and tavernas where one can enjoy the local specialities, as well as many shops where one can purchase hand–made objects created by local folk artists, and traditional hand–woven articles.

Continuing westwards, we come to *Axos* — which retains its ancient name. On the site of the ancient town, Late Minoan potsherds were discovered, as well as ruins of walls, archaic remains and clay female figurines. At the entrance to the town there is an important church of the 14th or 15th century, dedicated to Saint Irene.

From Axos, we follow the road which leads southwestwards to the village of *Zonianá*. Nearby, on an imposing site, is the *"Sendoni"* or, as the locals call it, "Sfendoni" *cave,* rich in stalactites and stalagmites. Its length is 550 m. and it covers an area of 3300 sq. metres.

The road continues towards the northwest and passes through various villages (Livadia, Aghios Ioannis, Aghios Mamas, Avdellas, Houmeri) and ar-

*Sendoni Cave, near the village
of Zoniana.
Impressive formations of
stalactites and stalagmites in
fantastic shapes. Some look
like ancient columns, others
resemble low hills.*

*The small
settlement of Lygaria
and the bay
of Aghia Pelagia
from the
picturesque scene.*

*Pp. 140-141:
The picturesque bay
of Aghia Pelagia.*

*Ammoudara.
Seaside holiday resort near
the town of Herakleion.*

rives at *Perama* (33.5 kms. from Anogheia).

From here a road to the north, 7 kms. in
length, leads to the new coastal national road between Herakleion and
Rethymnon, outside the village of *Panormos*. Four kilometres to the northwest of Perama lies *Melidóni* and, 1800
m. northwest of the village, the *cave* of
the same name, at an altitude of 300 m.
approximately. It is known also as "Ge-
rontospilia" or "Gerontospilios" (the old
man's cave). As is evidenced by the religious objects found here, the cave was
used as a place of worship from Minoan
to Roman times.

During the period of Turkish occupation (1823), about 400 inhabitants of
the village — most of them women and
children — suffered a tragic death
when they refused to surrender and
took refuge in this cave. The Turks set
fire to the entrance of the cave and all
those inside died of suffocation.

There is a monument at the cave, erected in memory of the martyred victims.

The cave consists of an enormous chamber (the Heroes' Chamber) with two
long and narrow passages to the right
and left, decorated with impressive
clusters of stalactites and stalagmites.
At the end of the left passage there is a
stepped precipice.

Seven and a half kilometres east of Perama, a road to the left leads to Aghiá
and Melidoni. From the 10th km. after
Perama, a road leads off in a southeasterly direction towards Gharazo,
Veni, Axos, Anogheia.

As our main road continues eastwards,
at the 23rd km. of the Perama–Herakleion road we come upon a detour to
the north, towards the Cretan sea and
the villages of *Alóides* and *Sisses*. We
continue on our main route, passing
through *Damásta* and, at the 33rd km.,
a fork to the north leads to the monastery of Aghios Pandeleimon and to
Fódele (7.5 kms. from the intersection),
a picturesque little village surrounded
by rich orange groves.

This is the native village of the great
painter Domenikos Theotokopoulos, or
"El Greco" (1545–1614). The house
where he was born is still standing.

Byzantine church at Fodele.

Near the village there is a church dedicated to the Presentation of the Virgin.
At a distance of three kilometres to the
north of Fodele, our road comes out onto
the new coastal national road between
Herakleion and Rethymnon. (From the
Fodele intersection to Herakleion: 26
kms.).

We follow the new national road and 4.5
kms. further on, a road to the left leads,
after 3.5 kms., to the picturesque bay of
Aghia Pelaghia — a lovely beach with
accommodation for tourists. Passing
through *Palaeokastro, Pantanassa, Linoperamata* — busy coastal settlements on the bay of Herakleion — we
come to an intersection before Ghazi.
Here we leave the national road and follow a coastal road to the left towards
the bay of *Ammoudára* and Herakleion.

Outside Linoperamata, there is a road
to the right of the national road which
leads north to *Rogdiá,* a charming village on a verdant slope. To the northwest of this village is the *monastery of
the Sabbathians,* standing remote and
solitary, in an idyllic setting. The
monastery has two churches, one dedicated to the Holy Virgin and the other
to Saint Anthony. The church of St. Anthony is 200 m. further along and part
of it is carved out of the rock.

8

HERAKLEION – RETHYMNON

Herakleion – Platanés – Arkadi monastery – Eléftherna. Return: Perivólia (Prassiés – Assomaton monastery – Amári).

Leaving Herakleion through the Chania Gate, we follow the new coastal national road to the west.

We pass the Ghazi intersection and continue towards the northwest for Linoperamata, Pantanassa, Palaeokastro, Aghia Pelaghia intersection (see route 7, in the opposite direction). We continue westwards towards the Fodele intersection (26 kms.) and Sisses (35 kms. from Herakleion). 12.5 kms. beyond Sisses, 48 kms. from Herakleion, a short detour to the right leads to the lovely coastal settlement of *Balí* built on a picturesque little bay, with sandy beaches, a clean sea, several hotels and rooms to rent, restaurants, seafood tavernas etc.

Not far from the settlement is the monastery of St. John the Baptist, dating from the 16th century.

At the 58 km. point on the Herakleion to Rethymnon national road just off the main road, lies *Panormos* (detour to the south towards Perama Melidoni. see route 7).

This is a seaside village, popular with tourists, offering hotel accommodation, tavernas, bars, discos etc. It is believed that, on this same spot, stood the ancient town of the same name, which was the port of Eleftherna. During the Venetian period, and up to the early 20th century, it was known as Kastelli. It has a strong fortress with seven tow-

ers and two gates, of which nothing remains today, as it was destroyed by Khair–ed–Din Barbarossa in 1538.

To the southwest of the village, at the site of Aghia Sophia, lie the ruins of an early Christian 5th century basilica with a wooden roof, believed to have been dedicated to Saint Sophia.

Our route continues westwards, along the coast. We pass through the village of *Stavromenos* (69 kms. from Herakleion), and here we join the old Herakleion to Rethymnon national road (Chani Alexandrou – Perama – Damasta – Marathos – Ghazi: route 7. South of Chani Alexandrou lies the picturesque village of *"Margarites,"* which has a long tradition of pottery–making).

Five hundred metres from Stavromenos, a left detour leads us to the *Arseni monastery*.

Further along the road to the west we come to the summer resorts of *Kambos Pighis* or *Pighianos Kambos,* and *Adelianos Kambos.*

At the 75th km., a flyover with a fork towards the southeast leads, after 17 kms., and after passing through the villages of Adele, Pighi, Loutra, Kyrianna, and Amnato, to the historic *monastery of Arkadi* (23 kms. southeast of Rethymnon), built on a hill with a magnificent view over the verdant area surrounding it. (A tourist pavillion operates outside the monastery).

Left: The two-aisled church of the Arkadi Monastery.

Above: The torso of the statue from Eleutherna (Herakleion Archaeological Museum).

The monastery is built like a fortress. It is surrounded by several buildings and its external walls are 1.2 m. thick.

The main entrance to the monastery is on the western side of the castle precinct, through the so–called Chania or Rethymnon Gate, which was destroyed in 1866 and rebuilt in 1870, on the same pattern as the original gate. This is where the monks' cells were situated, which communicated with the courtyard through a cloister, as in Catholic monasteries.

Other buildings within the precinct are the restored hostel, the *Trapeza* or refectory of the monastery, and the powder magazine. The south wing of the monastery houses a museum, containing many religious relics and icons. There is also an ossuary, where the bones of the dead heroes of the Arkadi holocaust are kept.

Almost at the centre of the precinct stands the monastery church, a basilica with a baroque facade and two naves — one of which is dedicated to the Transfiguration of Christ and the other to Saints Constantine and Helen. The woodcarved iconostasis was destroyed during the 1866 explosion. Parts of it are kept in the museum.

According to one theory, the monastery was founded in the 5th century by the Byzantine emperor, Arcadius, from whom it got its name.

According to another – which is probably the correct one – it was founded by a monk named Arcadius.

The church with its two naves was built in 1587 and its architectural style is a mixture of Renaissance, Gothic, Classical and Baroque elements.

The 16th and 17th centuries were a period of prosperity for the monastery: it had 300 or so monks, according to written testimonies of foreign travellers, important revenues and a rich library. It was a centre for the copying of manuscripts while, during the 18th century, it included a workshop for the fashioning and embroidering in gold of holy vestments.

After the Greek War of Independence of 1821, many Cretan guerilla fighters who were being hunted by the Turks, took refuge in the monastery. It thus became a meeting place for independence fighters, who used the monastery for their secret councils.

On November 7th, 1866, a Turkish force of 15,000 men besieged the monastery, and its leader demanded of the Abbot Gabriel to surrender the members of the revolutionary committee who were gathered there. At that time, apart from the members of the committee, 300 armed men and 600 or so women and children had also taken refuge in the monastery. When the Abbot refused, the Turks opened fire. Those entrenched in the monastery resisted fiercely for two days, but on November 9th, their resistance weakened and, in order not to surrender to the enemy, the fighters set fire to the powder magazines. In the explosion, all those in the monastery were killed and, with them, many Turks who had in the meantime forced their way into the monastery.

The "Arkadi holocaust", as this heroic sacrifice came to be called, is a landmark of immense importance in the history of the struggle of the Cretan people for freedom.

To the northeast of the Arkadi monastery, a road — half tarred, half dirt — leads to the village of Eléftherna. There is a road from Perama as well. (Old national road from Herakleion to Rethymnon). The village is situated on a hill which stands out amidst a fertile region.

Near the village are the ruins of the ancient town of the same name, which is also known as Apollonia. It is believed to have been founded during the Geometric period and to have flourished until Roman and early Byzantine times. It had a wall built with huge blocks of stone, an aqueduct and large reservoirs. On the northern side of the hill there stood a temple, which was believed to have been dedicated to the god Apollo, who was worshipped here. Sys-

tematic excavations were begun on this site in 1985.

We now return to the main road.

After the plain of Adele, the road passes through the coastal suburbs of Rethymnon: Platanes, Misiria and Perivolia, and leads to Rethymnon town, 80 kms. from Herakleion. From *Perivólia* (3 kms. east of Rethymnon) a fork on the left, leading southwards, passes through many picturesques villages and crosses the fertile valley of Amari, situated almost in the heart of the prefecture of Rethymnon. It leads to an interesting area with many Byzantine churches.

Among these villages we might mention: Prassiés, Thronos, Apostoli, the Asomaton monastery (which runs a farm school). A detour takes us to *Amári* (6 kms.), the capital of the province of the same name, while the road continues southeastwards towards Vizari, Fourfoura, Apodoulou.

Just before the last village, the site of a Late Minoan settlement and a vaulted tomb were discovered. Beyond the village of Apodoulou, the road branches out: the left fork leads to Kamares, Vrontissi monastery — Zaro (see route 6), while the right fork takes us to Aghia Galini on the coast.

The coastal settlement of Misiria, from where the road leads to the Amari valley.

Inscription from the Asomaton Monastery.
The Byzantine church of Aghia Paraskevi near the Asomaton Monastery.

AGHIOS NIKOLAOS

Capital of the Lasithi prefecture, Aghios Nikolaos is a modern town built on the northwestern point of the Mirabello bay. It is the administrative, cultural and communications centre of the prefecture and attracts many tourists because of its picturesque harbour and the many interesting sites of the surrounding area. It has many high quality hotels and rooms, of every kind and in a wide price range, as well as beautiful beaches, a good road network and frequent bus services linking it to destinations both within the prefecture and beyond it.

Today it is a cosmopolitan centre throbbing with life, with elegant shops, restaurants, tavernas, bars, discos etc., where one can spend unforgettable holidays and indulge in a wide variety of interesting and enjoyable activities.

Aghios Nikolaos is built on the site of the ancient town of Lato towards Kamara, which was a seaport of Lato Hetera (the Other Lato). It flourished during the 3rd century BC and, being an autonomous city, it minted its own coins. During the Roman and early Byzantine periods, it continued to flourish and is mentioned as a bishop's see in the 6th century AD.

After this time, our information concerning the town grows scant and we only find it mentioned again during the Venetian period, when the Venetian occupiers built the Mirabello (meaning "lovely view") fortress, on a hill near the sea - where the Prefecture headquarters are situated today- in order to protect the small port. Nothing remains of this fortress but its name,

Bottom: Tourist facilities
in the bay of Mirabello.
Right: The town of Aghios Nikolaos.

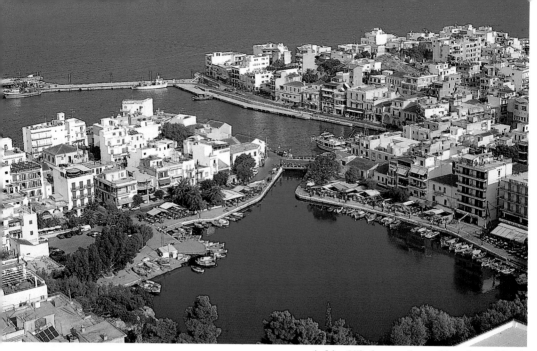

Aghios Nikolaos - where old and new blend harmoniously together.

which has now extended over the entire province and the bay which it once dominated. The fortress was destroyed by an earthquake in 1303, was rebuilt, was once more destroyed by pirates and rebuilt by the Venetians.

In 1645 the fortress was taken by the Turks, then recaptured by the Venetians who burnt it down. After that, it was no longer inhabited. At the same time, the Venetians had built another, more protected port, in the Elounda area, to the northwest, which they named "Porto di San Niccoló".

The town was deserted during the Turkish occupation, but its harbour still continued to be used, and was known as Mandraki.

During the later years of Turkish occupation, a small settlement grew up around the port, which took the name of Aghios Nikolaos from the old domed church with a single nave, dedicated to Saint Nicholas, which stood on the small peninsula in the harbour.

The "trademark" of Aghios Nikolaos is the Voulismeni lake in its middle, which is linked to the sea by a canal. This is a particularly picturesque part of the town, with many outdoor coffee-shops and restaurants all along the coast.

MUSEUMS

The town has an **Archaeological Museum** (68, Palaeologou street, tel. no.0841/24.943, 22.462 and 22.382), with rich and interesting exhibits from the excavations in the area.

There is also a noteworthy **Folk Art Museum** which occupies the ground floor of the Port Police building (tel. no. 25093), and includes beautiful samples of folk art — weaving, woodcarving — as well as local costumes and Byzantine icons.

The "Myrtos goddess", a characteristic example of Minoan art, of the Early Minoan period. (Archaeological Museum of Aghios Nikolaos).

Bronze "aryballos" (oil vial) of an athlete (1st century AD). Archaeological Museum of Aghios Nikolaos.

Characteristic painted decoration on clay. Archaeological Museum of Aghios Nikolaos.

TOUR STARTING
FROM AGHIOS NIKOLAOS

Aghios Nikolaos – Kritsá – Lató – back to Aghios Nikolaos – Elounda – Plaka – Spinalonga.

At a distance of 11 kilometres south-west of Aghios Nikolaos lies the picturesque village of Kritsá, built amphi-theatrically on a hill. It is renowned for the quality of its handwoven articles. About one kilometre before we come to the village, at Logari, we find the church of Panaghiá or Kerá. It has three naves: the central one is dedicated to the Dormition of the Virgin and the other two to Saint Anne and Saint Anthony respectively.

The church has very important and well–preserved wall–paintings dating from the 14th and 15th centuries, interesting from the point of view of themes and style.

Three kilometres to the north of Kritsá, at Kontaratos, lie the ruins of the ancient Doric city of *Lató Hetera.* It flourished between the 7th and the 3rd centuries BC and was protected by two a-cropoles, between which it lay. This archaeological site was excavated by the French School of Archaeology, and includes an agora, a number of public buildings and several houses.

We return to Aghios Nikolaos by the same route.

From there we drive north, along the coast, which attracts many visitors and where a number of hotels have been built.

At the 9 km. point, we come to *Schisma,* a seaside settlement very popular with tourists, situated near the scant remains of the Greco–Roman city of *Elounda,* the greater part of which is buried under the sea.

Opposite us we can see the long and narrow *Spinalonga peninsula,* separated from the mainland by a canal (Poros canal — opened in 1897 by French sailors). Today, a bridge spans the canal.

To the east of the seaside village of Plaka and exactly opposite the northern point of the peninsula, lies the *rocky islet of Spinalonga or Kalydon.*
In 1579, on this little island and above the ruins of the ancient acropolis, the Venetians built a strong fortress to protect the harbour of Elounda. Ruins of this fortress, which is one of the most important in Crete and was plentifully supplied with ammunition and cannon, still survive today.

The Spinalonga fortress, together with those of Souda and Gramvousa, were the only ones on the whole island which did not fall into the hands of the Turks when the latter took Crete in 1669.

These fortresses remained under Venetian domination for another half century or so, and only in 1715 did they capitulate and pass into Turkish hands.

Caïques link the islet of Spinalonga with Aghios Nikolaos, Elounda and Plaka.

As we continue on the coastal road towards the north, we come to *Elounda,* 10.5 kilometres from Aghios Nikolaos

Spinalonga - with the ruins of the once mighty Venetian fortress.

156

The church of Panaghia Kera near Kritsa, with its three aisles.

Left: Murals of the 14th-15th century from Panaghia Kerá.

and 1.5 kilometres west of the seaside settlement of Schisma. This is one of the most developed holiday resorts in Greece. It disposes of a large number of beds in excellent hotels, with all the modern comforts and amenities and the possibility to indulge in a variety of sports. There are also many shops and restaurants, tavernas, bars, discos, etc., which attract thousands of visitors all the year round.

Further north, opposite the northern-most point of the Spinalonga peninsula and its fortified islet, lies the fishing village of *Plaka* (14 kms. from Aghios Nikolaos). Here, there are tavernas offering fresh fish and seafood. Plaka is at a distance of 5 kilometres from Elounda.

Pp. 158-159: Cosmopolitan Elounda.

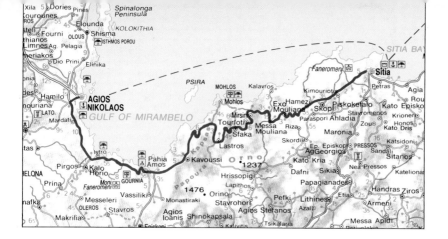

AGHIOS NIKOLAOS – SITEIA

Aghios Nikolaos – Mardáti – Istro – Gourniá – Pacheiá Ammos – Kavousi – Lastros – Sfáka – Mochlós – Myrsini – Mouliáná – Hamézi – Siteia.

From the lovely capital of the Lasithi prefecture we carry on southwards towards Mardáti, Istro and Gourniá (18 kms. southeast of Aghios Nikolaos).

Visit of Gourniá

An entire Minoan settlement was discovered on this important archaeological site: houses, streets, and a large structure on the top of the hill, which was probably the residence of the overlord of the region. The acme of the city's development has been dated to 1600–1400 BC approximately, and its decline coincides with its destruction, perhaps by fire, around 1200 BC. To the north of the small palace, a sanctuary, containing many objects of worship, was uncovered. A great number of household vessels and tools were also brought to light. The stepped, stone–paved streets of the settlement, the foundations of houses and, on the hill, remains of the small palace, are still to be seen today.

Continuing eastwards, on the Aghios Nikolaos — Siteia road, we pass through the pretty village of *Pacheiá Ammos* (21 kms. from Aghios Nikolaos), nestled deep in Mirabello bay, with a magnificent beach and crystal-clear waters. This is the narrowest point of the island.

Left: The archaeological site of Gournes.
Above: The Venetian Fortress of Siteia.

From the 22nd kilometre, to the right, a road leads to Ierapetra (14 km.). The main road continues towards the northeast, climbing upwards. We pass through the village of *Kavousi* (26 kms.), beyond which is the site called Plátanos (31.5 kms.), from which we can enjoy a panoramic view. At the 33rd km., we come to the first detour for Mochlos then to the village of *Lástros* (36 kms.) – with its Byzantine church dedicated to Saint George — and finally to *Sfaka* (40 kms.), where there is a second detour for Mochlos.

Móchlos is a little fishing village, with an islet opposite, which was believed to have been linked to the mainland in Minoan times. In the western part of the islet, many mass chamber tombs were discovered, which yielded rich finds, mainly gold jewellery and very beautiful pottery (Archaeological Museums of Herakleion and of Aghios Nikolaos).

On another islet, called *Pseira,* on the eastern end of Mirabello bay, a Minoan settlement was found.

Wall–paintings in relief adorned the wall of one of the houses of the settlement (Archaeological Museum of Herakleion).

We continue eastwards on the main road, passing through picturesque villages: Myrsini (third detour for Mochlos), Mesa Mouliana, Exo Mouliana. At the 57.5 km. to the right a detour leads, one kilometre later, to the *Minoan House of Hamezi,* a pre–historic fortress–like circular building or, according to others, a peak sanctuary.

At *Hamézi,* 59 kilometres from Aghios

Above: Istros bay.
Right: The picturesque town of Siteia.

Nikolaos, it is worth visiting the *folk art museum,* which has noteworthy exhibits, among which a rare kind of loom and its accessories.

At the end of our journey we arrive at *Siteia* (69 kms. from Aghios Nikolaos), a picturesque harbour, built amphitheatrically on the western side of the bay of Siteia, on the site of ancient Eteia.

East of Siteia stood the Venetian fortress, of which only a few ruins still survive today.

The modern town was built after 1870 while, during the two previous centuries, it had remained uninhabited.

In the *Siteia Archaeological Museum* (tel. no. 0843/23.917), is exhibited an important collection of pottery from Aghia Fotia and Mochlos, Pseira, Palaikastro and Zacros. Among the exhibits there are also clay tablets inscribed in Linear A from the palace at Zacros and a grape-pressing machine – unique in its kind – with authentic accessories, from the same palace. The Greco–Roman collection consisting of pots and oil–lamps is also important. The *Folk Art Museum* of the town houses many exhibits, mainly hand–woven articles, embroidery, folk costumes, traditional furniture, household utensils, a loom, etc.

Not far from the town, to the north, is the airport. There are direct flights to Athens and to the island of Karpathos.

163

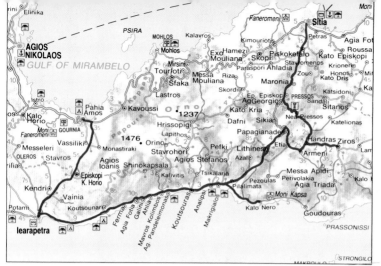

11

Siteia – Piskokéfalo – Praisós – Handrás – Ziros Arméni – Etiá – Lithines – Pilalimata – (Moni Kapsá) – Makrygialos – Ierapetra – Episkopi – Vassiliki – Pacheiá Ammos.

Starting out from Siteia, we take a southerly direction towards the Libyan sea, coming to *Pisokéfalo* 3.4 kms. from our starting point.

A right detour to the southwest leads, after a drive of 5 kilometres, to Achladia, where a Minoan villa and a vaulted tomb were discovered. Continuing along the main road, we pass through the villages of Maronia and Epano Episkopi.

Eleven kilometres from Siteia, the road branches out. The main road to the right leads to Aghios Georgios, Sykia, Papagiannádes, while the road to the left takes us, after 4.5 kms. to *Nea Praisos* and from there to the archaeological site of Praisos, the city of the Eteocretans, who were the genuine descendants of the Minoans. The city was very powerful and built on three hills, on each of which was an acropolis. It was surrounded by a wall — except for the third hill which was outside the walls and was called Altar Hill.

The city had two harbours, one to the north on the Cretan sea, called Eteia (Siteia), and one to the south on the Libyan sea, called Steles. After a long-drawn-out struggle, the powerful opponent of Praisos, Dorian Ierapytna, prevailed and destroyed Praisos (146 BC).

Left: Aghia Fotia.
Above: Praisos. High up on the acropolis.

The excavations at Praisos, which were begun in 1884 by Federico Halbherr, brought to light the first Eteocretan inscription and a multitude of clay figurines. After 1901, excavations were continued by the British School of Archaeology which revealed that the ruins of today do not belong to the city of the Eteocretans, but to a powerful city of the historic – Hellenic period, while Eteocretan Praisos was built on a site not far from these ruins.

On the first hill, which was also the centre of the town, a Hellenistic palace with a drainage system was uncovered. There was also a stone basin to collect water and an olive–press.

On the third hill many bronze and clay offerings were found, shields, helmets, breastplates, and three extremely important Eteocretan inscriptions, carved "boustrophedon" ("as the ox plows", i.e. from right to left and then from left to right) on limestone tablets. In this area various vaulted tombs were also excavated.

From Praisos we continue south towards *Handrás,* from where we take the road to the east towards *Ziros.* Here, worth seeing is the church of Aghia Paraskevi, with its layers of frescoes.

From Ziros, we return to Handrás and continue southwards towards the village of Armeni, to the west of which, just before we come to the main road, is *Etiá*, where there is a three–storey Venetian villa, a representative example of Creto–Venetian architecture.

the coast the landscape is green and pleasant and there are many greenhouses where early fruit and vegetables are grown.

We pass through the villages of Analipsi, Koutsoura, Mavro Kolymbo, Achlia, Galini, Aghia Fotia, Ferma. Then, after Ferma and 9 kms. before Ierapetra, a detour to the right towards the north leads to *Aghios Ioannis.* At the beginning of the turn-off very near the main road, at Koutsounari, there are places to stay which are traditional and picturesque.

All along the coast from Makrygialo to Ierapetra, a good number of tourist complexes have been built.

From Ierapetra (62 kms. from Siteia), we leave the coast road which leads westwards towards Myrtos, and follow a fork to the right northwards to *Pacheiá Ammos* (see route 10). This part, between Ieraptera and Pacheia Ammos, is the narrowest part of the island, where there are only 14 kilometres of road between the Cretan and the Libyan seas.

We pass through Episkopi and, after 5.5 kms., to the north, on the left of the road, we come to *Vassiliki* (24 kms. from Aghios Nikolaos, 12 kms. from Ierapetra).

During the excavations near the village — which are still going on — Minoan houses were uncovered, and among them the so-called "House on the Hill", belonging to the Pre-palatial period. Here, too, were found the characteristic pots of the "Vassiliki" type (Archaeological Museum of Herakleion and of Aghios Nikolaos).

Our route brings us to the Aghios Nikolaos – Siteia national road, at the 22nd km. point.

We leave the main road and continue southwards towards *Lithines* and *Pilalimata.*

Thirty–three kilometres from Siteia, there ia a dirt road to the left, parallel to the coast, which leads to Kalá Nerá and to the *Monastery of Kapsá,* (7 kms. from the intersection), which is built on the side of a steep ravine with a cave. It is dedicated to Saint John the Forerunner (Aghios Ioannis o Prodromos). To the west of the monastery is the Pervolakia gorge.

It is believed that the monastery was founded in the mid–15th century. In 1471 it was destroyed by pirates and abandoned. It was later restored by a monk, who added a nave to the church and dedicated it to the Holy Trinity.

At the 34.5 km. point, we come to *Makrygialos,* a beautiful seaside settlement with clear waters, a magnificent beach — one of the longest in Crete — modern tourist accommodation, many tavernas, restaurants, bars, discos, etc.

Near the village, a Minoan villa was discovered, several finds of which are exhibited in the Archaeological Museum of Aghios Nikolaos.

We continue westwards towards Ierapetra. For 27 kilometres, our road runs parallel to the coast and passes through many seaside spots with small sheltered coves and transparent waters. Along

12

Siteia – Aghia Fotiá – Toplou monastery – Vaï (Palm tree grove) – Itanos – Palaikastro – Kato Zakros.

From Siteia we drive eastwards, and 4.5 kms. along the road, we come to a detour to the right, leading in a southerly direction towards Roussa Ekklesia, Kryoneri and Mitato.

At the sixth kilometre on the main road lies *Aghia Fotiá*. Near the village an entire necropolis was discovered, with many chamber and pit tombs of the Early Minoan period. Among the rich finds in the graves were blades, stone and bronze artifacts and a great number of pots in a variety of shapes and sizes (Archaeological Museum of Aghios Nikolaos and of Siteia).

Nine kilometres east of Aghia Fotiá, a detour to the left, leading north, takes us, after 3.5 kms., to the historical fortress-monastery of Toplou (also called Panaghia Akrotiriani), one of the richest and most important monasteries in Crete.

It is believed that the monastery was built in the 15th century. It was destroyed by an earthquake in 1612 and rebuilt, then parts of it crumbled and were restored by the monks with funds provided by the faithful.

It is square–shaped and surrounded by a strong wall, 10 metres in height. It was provided with cannon with which to repulse pirate raids. The main building covers an area of about 800 sq. m. and is three storeys high. The entrance is through the Wheel Gate, which was so called because its great weight made it necessary for it to be pulled open and

Left: the historic fortress-monastery of Toplou.
Top: Part of the icon "Great art thou O Lord".

shut by means of a wheel. Set in, on the inside lintel, is a marble plaque in relief, showing a carved cross borne by two dolphins. The Italianate belfry stands separate from the church, which has two naves. The northern and older nave is dedicated to the Birthday of the Holy Virgin, and the southern one to Saint John the Divine.

The walls are adorned with well–preserved 14th century murals. Only very few of the monastery's precious relics still survive today, as the monastery was repeatedly plundered by the Turks. There are several interesting icons, among which a most important one painted by Ioannis Kornaros in 1770, entitled "Great art Thou, o Lord".

An inscribed plaque of the 2nd century BC, built in on the face of the church, is of great archaeological value. It was discovered among the ruins of ancient Itanos and brought here. During the Turkish occupation, the monastery functioned as a school for the Greek children of the region, while the monks themselves actively took part in the struggle against the Turks, or offered refuge to freedom fighters who were being hunted.

In 1870, a school was founded, which operated until fairly recently while, in the difficult years of the German occupation, the monks once again were in the forefront of the resistance, setting up a radio transmitter to serve the needs of the movement.

We continue on our route towards the northeast and come to *Vaï* after 7 kilometres. Not very far (1.5 kms) to the east,

Left: Palaikastro.

Right and pp.172-173:
The famous palm tree grove, Vai.
Crystal-clear sea,
golden sand and ancient palm trees.

we find the famous *Palm Forest.* The crystal–clear sea, the magnificent golden sand, lend this beach, which is unique in Greece, a special enchantment which attracts thousands of visitors. The greatest part of the palm tree grove is fenced in and is only open to visitors from sunrise to sunset, while free camping and overnight stays are strictly forbidden.

After the short detour to the Palm Forest, the road continues northwards for another 1.5 kilometres, and comes to the site where *Ancient Itanos* was situated, and which today is known as Erimoupolis "the deserted city").

To the east is the islet of Elassa.

Itanos was inhabited since Minoan times and until the 15th century, when the town was destroyed by pirates and its inhabitants fled inland for safety. During the period of its prosperity, it was an important harbour and a commercial centre for the transportation of goods from Crete to the East. On the site were found inscribed tombstones of the Pre–Christian period, the most important of which is the one encased in the wall of the Toplou monastery.

From Itanos we descend southwards by the same road to Vaï and, shortly after-

wards, we take a left fork which leads us, 6 kilometres further on, to *Palaikastro* (19 kms. from Siteia). The ruins in the area indicate that, near Palaikastro, there used to be a town which was inhabited from the Mycenean to the Hellenistic period.

To the southeast of the village, at *Roussolakkos,* excavations carried out in the early years of our century by the British School of Archaeology, uncovered an entire Minoan settlement traversed by a main street, with smaller streets running perpendicularly to it, and separating the settlement into neighbourhoods. Almost the entire area is covered, today, for protection, so that only a small part is visible. On the same spot, ruins were discovered, which were believed to have belonged to the Sanctuary of the Dictaean Zeus.

Further south, on the top of *Petsofá* hill, an outdoor peak sanctuary of the Middle Minoan period was discovered. Here were found very interesting male and female clay figurines, measuring 10–17 cm. in height, and with their arms held in a position of prayer. The figurines were votive offerings to some deity — probably a female one — which was worshipped in this sanctuary.

Clay figurines of wild and domestic animals were also discovered here.

From Palaikastro we continue southwards, to Langada, Kamara, Hochlakiés, Azokeramo, where the road takes a westerly direction toward Kellaria and then turns south again for Adravastoi and Zakros (39 kms. from Siteia). At a distance of 8 kms. southeast, in a little sheltered bay on the easternmost point of the island, lies *Kato Zakros,* where the ruins of Ancient Zakros were uncovered.

Kato Zacros. View of the archaeological site.

Visit of Kato Zakros

In the western corner of a small valley, the fourth largest Minoan palace was discovered. The study of the area and of the numerous finds proves the existence here of a populous Minoan city, which, because of its geographical position, served as a commercial harbour and as a transit station for the ships travelling to the African or Asian coasts. It is believed that this was where the goods coming from the Asian ports and Egypt were unloaded, to be conveyed thereafter to their destinations, the large Minoan centres of Knossos, Phae-

stos and Mallia. As the excavations show, the wider region, to the north and west of the palace, had been inhabited since prehistoric times and up to Roman times. Ruins of Roman houses, at Kali Strata, confirm the existence of a small Roman settlement. Also, at the sites known as Farangas ton Nekron and Traostalos, prehistoric cemeteries were found.

In 1901, the British archaeologist, D.G. Hogarth, excavated the flank of a hill to the northeast of the palace, and discovered about ten houses of the Late

Minoan period, and important artifacts of the Mycenean period.

Sixty years later, N. Platon began systematic excavations on the site, which are still in progress today.

Initially, he discovered two building complexes which were believed to have constituted a manor–farmhouse. Then, led by various potsherds which local peasants had found in their fields, he came upon the ruins of the palace.

The size of the structure, its careful construction, the variety of shapes and the richness of decoration of the pottery found here, the spacious rooms, the quantity of storerooms, the colonnades, the labyrinthine disposition of the various areas, the workshops, all testified to this being a palace. The kings of Zacros prospered, as a result of their commerce with the lands of the Asian and African coasts, from which they obtained precious raw materials such as ivory and gold. These were then used, together with local materials, by the palace craftsmen, to produce various vessels or decorative objects, a large number of which came to light in the excavations.

The palace was built around 1600 BC and was destroyed around 1450 BC.

Under the eastern wing, ruins of a Pre–palatial complex were found.

Here, too, as in other Minoan palaces, there is a central court, around which the structure developed, in labyrinthine form. It has two storeys and, according to the archaeologists, it appears to have covered an area of 8000 sq. metres, and to have comprised more than 300 apartments.

Entrance to the palace is effected through the northeastern side, from which a flagstone–paved road led to the harbour.

The central court is surrounded by four wings of apartments, each having a different function. In the western wing is the *ceremonial hall,* the roof of which was held up by polychrome columns, with an interior *polythyron* and light-well. Only the bases of the columns, and a few fragments of the frescoes which adorned the walls have survived.

In this room, many religious objects were found, among which a rhyton with the depiction of a peak sanctuary, and another in the shape of a bull's head (Archaeological Museum of Herakleion).

This hall communicates with the *banquet hall* through a triple door. Here, a great number of vessels, wine pitchers and cups were found, as well as parts of a fresco in relief, which is exhibited in the Archaeological Museum of Herakleion. Through the western side of the ceremonial hall, we come to the *sanctuary proper* which comprises eleven rooms: the priests' rooms, the room where the religious vessels were kept, the archives room — where tablets in Linear A script were found — the central sanctuary, the depository, the lustral basin — here a veined marble amphora was discovered — the treasury, containing a great number of ritual vessels and sacred symbols made of various precious materials.

The *storerooms* are in the northern section of the west wing. These contained various vessels of excellent quality and many pithoi (large jars).

To the west of the sanctuary are the *workshops.*

The east wing housed the sumptuous royal apartments. The *queen's chamber* communicates through a corridor with the room called the *bath.*

To the east of the royal quarters there is a large square room with a circular cistern, which is believed to have been encircled by a colonnade.

On the south side of the basin is a *spring and further south another spring* and a *well.* In the south wing were the craftsmen's workshops.

In the north wing were the servants quarters and a large room with columns, called the *kitchen* because of the cooking utensils found in it.

On the hill to the north of the palace, the houses which were discovered are believed to have belonged to the nobility and officials of the royal court.

The archaeological site of Kato Zakros is situated in the crook of a small bay with a marvellous beach and a lovely, clear sea.

*Rhyton made of rock crystal
from the excavations at Zakros.
(Archaeological Museum of Herakleion)*

*A stone rhyton depicting a peak sanctuary.
The most important stone jar of Zakros.
(Archaeological Museum of Herakleion)*

RETHYMNON

History of the town

Present–day Rethymnon is built on the site of ancient Rithymna, as the finds of a cemetery of the Late Minoan period, discovered in the Mastaba quarter, show.

The town flourished during Mycenean times. In the 3rd century AD, for some unknown reason, it lost its importance, and is only mentioned as a large village. However, Rithymna retained its autonomy and independence, as is evidenced by the coins which, as a free city, it continued to mint. During the Byzantine period the town continued to be inhabited, and parts of Roman and Byzantine mosaics have been found.

The Venetian period, also, was a time of great prosperity for Rithymna, as the Venetians used its harbour as an intermediate stop between Herakleion and Chania, and as an administrative centre for the area. Thus, Rithymna developed into one of the three most important towns in Crete. It retained its Greek char-

acter more than the other two large towns, even though it did come under Venetian influence, and it attracted several Cretans of noble descent. In its capacity as the most important centre in the region, it became the seat of the "Rettore" — the Venetian governor.

Rethymnon suffered raids, fires and plunder by the terrible Khair-ed–Din Barbarossa and other pirates, and was finally taken by the Turks in 1646. The Venetians and Greeks entrenched themselves in the Fortezza, but after a siege of 22 days, they were forced to surrender.

During the period of Ottoman rule, Rethymnon fell into decline as, besides, did the other towns. During the difficult years of the struggle for independence, its inhabitants were actively involved and, as a result, many of its freedom–fighters were executed.

In 1897, the Russian army took Rethymnon and held it until 1909. In 1913, it became part of Greece, together with the rest of Crete. During the German occupation, the Rethymniots took an act-

ive part in the resistance against fascism.

Visit of the town

Rethymnon is the capital of the prefecture of the same name. It lies between the other two large towns — Herakleion to the east (at a distance of 80 kms.) and Chania to the west (at a distance of 60 kms.).

Rethymnon is a blend of modernity and old-time dignity and charm. It has a population of about 20,000 inhabitants, and is the administrative and commercial centre of the prefecture, as well as a communications centre. It is well provided with tourist facilities and prides itself on its cultural activity and its significant presence in the general cultural life of the island, much of which is centred around the Faculty of Letters of the University of Crete, established here.

Artistic events are regularly organized, as are exhibitions, plays, concerts and lectures.

Rethymnon is linked by bus with the main towns and villages of the prefecture and also with Herakleion and Chania. There is also a regular year–round boat service linking Rethymnon with the port of Piraeus, but the town also makes use of the nearby port of Souda. Rethymnon has no airport, but it does have regular connections with the Chania airport.

Its lovely coastline, splendid beaches to the east, the local colour which, in several nooks and neighbourhoods, has survived untouched, the picturesque little streets in the old part of town, the contrasts and surprises we meet here, the variety of interests the town caters for, make Rethymnon a magnet which attracts a great number of visitors.

Among the worthwhile sights, the following, in particular, should be mentioned:

The Fortress or "Fortezza." This was built on the Palaeokastro hill by the Venetians, between 1573 and 1580, in order to strengthen the defences of the

Rethymnon. The Venetian castle, or "Fortezza".

harbour, which was so important to them. It had strong walls and four bastions. Inside the fortress there were public buildings, barracks, storerooms for ammunition and an army hospital. Today, the only surviving parts are the reconstructed walls, the cisterns and a mosque with a large dome, which was initially a church dedicated to Saint Nicholas. The Fortezza fell into the hands of the Turks in 1646.

The Loggia. The Loggia of Rethymnon cannot compare in grandeur with that of Herakleion. It is a handsome square

Venetian building dating from the end of the 16th or the beginning of the 17th century. It has three semi–circular arches on three of its sides, while the southern side has no opening. The Loggia was used as a place of meeting and recreation for the nobility during the Venetian period. When the Turks took over the town, they turned the Loggia into a mosque and built a minaret on its western side.

The Rimondi Fountain. This is an interesting Venetian monument with which the "Rettore" of Rethymnon, Ri-

Rethymnon. The old aristocratic quarters with their genuine traditional flavour blend with the pleasant modern town.

mondi, endowed the town in 1629. It has four elegant columns with elaborate capitals, which hold up an epistyle with a Latin inscription on it. Between the two interior columns are carved the armorial bearings of the Rimondi family. The fountain is adorned with three heads, from the mouths of which the water flows.

The Church of Saint Francis: interesting architecture and sculptured decoration.

The Turkish School: it is situated next to the church of Saint Francis. An inscription on one of its entrances indicates that it was built in 1796.

The Church of Our Lady of the Angels (Mikri Panaghia): this is a Roman Catholic church in the Old Town. It was built during the last years of Venetian rule.

Idyllic views of the Rethymnon sea front.

The Rimondi fountain (1629), an elegant Venetian monument.

The Cathedral of the Presentation of the Holy Virgin to the Temple.
The Bishop's Palace: This is a neo–classical building situated on the south side of the cathedral.
The Prefecture: this is a two–storey neo–classical building in Heroön Polytechniou square.
The Mosques: *Nerantzes* (once the Roman Catholic church of Santa Maria), *Kara Mousa Pasha* (formerly the Venetian monastery of Aghia Varvara, it now houses the Ephoreia of Byzantine Antiquities), the mosque of the *Megali Porta,* and finally, *Beli Pasha* in the Mastabas quarter.
Also worth noticing are many *facades of Venetian houses* in the Old Town.

MUSEUMS

Archaeological Museum of Rethymnon

(tel. no. 0831/29975)
It contains most important finds. Among them: figurines, jewellery, tools, spearheads of Neolithic times from the Gerani cave and the Ellenes Amariou cave.
It also includes ceramics of the Late Minoan period from Mastabas in Rethymnon and from the cemetery at Armeni, also sealstones, jewellery, sarcophagi, goddesses in worshipping stance, from various excavated sites in the prefecture.
A small Egyptian collection, red–figured vessels, Hellenistic and Roman statues are also exhibited, as is an important collection of coins of various periods and regions.

Historical and Folk Art Museum of Rethymnon (tel. 23.667). It houses a collection of handwoven items, paintings, as well as various folk art exhibits.

Folk Art Collection of the Lyceum Club of Greek Women (tel. no. 29.572). Here are exhibited collections of local costumes and jewellery. Also included is a large number of embroidered work and handwoven articles, as well as woodwork and pottery.

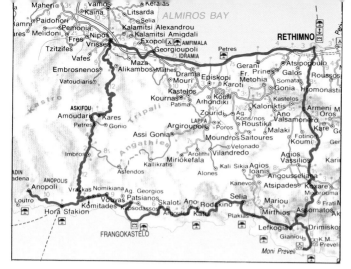

STARTING OUT FROM RETHYMNON

Rethymnon – Georgioupolis – Kourna lake – Vrysses – Askyfou – Imbros – Komitades – Chora Sfakion – Anopolis – Frangocastello – Rodakino – Selia – Lefkogeia – Preveli Monastery – Koxaré – Armeni – Rethymnon.

We take the national road from Rethymnon (new coastal road) in a westerly direction towards Chania, following the coast. Three kilometres further to the west, a detour leads south to the villages of Atsipopoulo, Prines, Gonia.

Further west along the new national road (7 kms. from Rethymnon) we come to a flyover towards Gerani, where an interesting cave with stalactites and stalagmites was discovered, containing important archaeological finds.

On the main route, 14.5 kms. further on, we come to an intersection leading southwards towards Episkopi and *Argyroupolis*. The latter occupies the site of the Doric town of *Lappa*, of which there are only scant remains today. Seven kilometres west of Argyroupolis lies *Asi Goniá*, a lovely village amid lush vegetation, built on a spot not easily accessible — which, is why it was a refuge for freedom–fighters during the Ottoman occupation. The inhabitants are herdsmen who retain their traditional pastoral customs and celebrate the local feast–days.

We continue along the new coastal national road for another 7.5 kms. westwards and, just before *Georgoupolis*, we

Left: Georgioupolis.
Above: Lake Kournas.

come to an intersection with a road to the south for *Kourna*. Here is where the only lake on Crete, *lake Kourna*, is to be found, with the impressive *White Mountains* in the background.

We return to the intersection with the national road and continue right for approximately another 500 metres to *Georgoupolis*. This is a seaside village in Almyros bay, offering accommodation for tourists and a lovely beach.

We have now left the new national road and follow the old national road towards *Vrysses*, a village with many springs and brooks and lush vegetation.

Vrysses is at a point where several roads meet.

We take the road leading southwards towards Chora Sfakion. This passes through Alikambos, *Askyfou* — on the plateau of the same name, at an altitude of 720 m. — Kares, Ammoudari, Petres (villages known for the heroic struggles of the people of the region of Sfakia against the Turks), and Imbros or Nimbros — the highest village of the area, built at an altitude of 780 metres, on a small plateau with a magnificent view of the Libyan sea.

We begin our descent. The road passes through the Nimbros gorge, with its wild and sheer walls. It is 6–7 kms. in length and its width at certain points is only 2 metres, while the height of its vertical sides is over 300 metres. It is one of the most impressive, as well as one of the narrowest, gorges in Crete and, in some parts, its walls are so close together that it seems like a tunnel.

Our road passes at a great height along the western side of the gorge. Further south, a right fork leads, after 3 kms., to Chora Sfakion and ends up in Anopolis. *Chora Sfakion,* 40 kms. from Vrysses, is a small harbour built in a steep, barren and inaccessible area on a rocky coast.

The fact that the village was in such an isolated position, approachable with difficulty both by land and by sea, was responsible, in great measure, for the stubborn, proud and unsubmissive character of the people of Sfakia.

During the Venetian period, the inhabitants were active in shipping and commerce and were very wealthy, owning their own ships and their own fine mansions. The village was one of the most prosperous in Crete. The foreign rulers were never able to impose their absolute domination over the town.

Around 1530, the Venetians built a fortress on the hill which is today known as Castelli. However, it only had one tower, and only served as the residence of the "provleptis". Today, very few of the remains of this fortress can still be seen. During the early years of Ottoman rule, the people of Sfakia continued their shipping activities and their wealth increased accordingly. They lived almost as free people, since the Turks avoided approaching this wild and inaccessible area. This was where a great many insurrections started during the struggle for freedom from Ottoman rule. After an unsuccessful revolution, the village was destroyed and many freedom–fighters, including the leader of the revolt, suffered a martyr's death. (1770).

The people of Sfakia also took part in the resistance movement against the Germans. On May 31st, 1941, after the Battle of Crete and the establishment on the island of the forces of occupation, the local people helped in the escape of the Australian and New Zealand troops who had remained on the island as a rear–guard.

The tiny harbour of Sfakia vibrates with life in the summer, when the caïques from Aghia Roumeli bring in hikers who have crossed the Samaria gorge. (See Route 17). This is where the hikers board the KTEL buses or private coaches which will take them back to Chania or Rethymnon.

One or two weekly services, by a small boat, link Chora Sfakion throughout the year with the island of *Gavdos* opposite, in the Libyan sea.

The village disposes of a limited number of beds for visitors in a small hotel, a pension and rooms for rent.

To the northwest of Chora Sfakion lies *Anopolis,* built on approximately the same site as the ancient town of the same name. Its history is similar to that of neighbouring Chora. It was a revolutionary centre during Venetian rule, as well as later during Ottoman rule. Its inhabitants used the nearby harbour of *Loutro,* a few kilometres to the south, in a sheltered bay, for their shipping activities.

On March 25th 1770, the rebel leader, Daskaloyiannis from Anopoli, raised the flag of the revolution against the Turks, inciting the chieftains from Sfakia to revolt. This revolution was drowned in blood, Daskaloyiannis was executed, and all the villages in the Sfakia area were destroyed.

We return to the crossroads with the road descending to the south (at the 37th km.) from Vrysses, and continue eastwards, following the southern coast. We pass through the villages of Komitades (at the point where the three roads meet — the village has two noteworthy Byzantine churches, that of Aghioi Apostoloi and Aghios Georgios), then through Vraskas, Vouvas, Nomikiana, Patsianos.

Here there is a fork to the right which leads, after approximately 2 kms., to *Frangocastello,* with its impressive fortress and enchanting beaches.

The fortress was built by the Venetians in 1371, in a lonely spot, with no settlement ("burgo") around it, and was in-

Impressive Frangocastello, built by the Venetians in 1371.

tended to protect this part of the southern coast from raids and to put down the uprisings of the local population.

The people of Sfakia called it Frangocastello, that is "fortress of the Franks". It is rectangular in shape, with strong walls and a square tower in each corner. It is similar in construction to the Ierapetra fortress.

Above its gate there is a carved lion of Saint Mark, and to the left and right, in relief, the crowns of Venetian noblemen. The buildings within the castle precinct are Turkish, built on Venetian foundations. Near the castle, towards the sea, the ruins of a church of Saint Haralambos can still be seen.

After Patsianos, we continue eastwards towards Kapsodasos, Skaloti (before Skaloti, another detour to the right leads back to Frangocastello), Argoules, Ano Rodakino, Kato Rodakino — in an area full of olive groves.

From Rodakino, a road of two kilometres in length descends southwards, towards the beach of Korakas and the little seaside settlement of Polyrizo. We continue towards Selia, Myrthos, Mariou and Lefkogeia. From Selia and from Lefkogeia there are roads leading to the lovely seaside settlement of *Plakias,* deep in the bay of the same name. It attracts many visitors on holiday or on day trips during the summer, and offers accommodation in hotels and rooms to rent, as well as restaurants, tavernas, etc. The beaches of Damnoni, Ammoudi, Skinaria are quieter.

From Plakias, there are excursions by caïque to Frangocastello, Limni Preveli, Aghia Galini and Chora Sfakion.

From Lefkogeia, a road (half–tarred, half–dirt) leads eastwards and then southwards to the *Preveli monastery,* south of the village of Asomatos. This is a 16th or 17th century monastery. Its church, of a later date, is dedicated to

Saint John the Divine and is built on an enchanting spot — a hill with a superb view towards the Libyan sea.

A dirt road leads to the Preveli coast, at the mouth of the Kourtaliotis river. Just before the point where the Kourtaliotis meets the sea, its waters form a small lake. This coast and the area around it is one of the most idyllic spots in Crete.

The monastery, which acquired a huge extent of landed property thanks to the offerings of its faithful, has twenty cells, a guest house, a library and a museum, where vestments, holy vessels and important religious relics are exhibited. On a fountain outside, there is a carved inscription bearing the date 1701.

Inside the church there is a very valuable silver chandelier, a Holy Cross covered in gold and inlaid with precious stones, which is believed to perform miracles, an intricately carved episcopal throne and pulpit.

As is the case with most of the monasteries of Crete, Preveli played a very important role in the struggle against the Turks and during the German occupation, offering refuge to a number of Greek freedom–fighters and to allied soliders who took part in the Battle of Crete.

We return to Asomatos and continue northwards towards *Koxarés,* through the impressive *Kourtaliotis gorge,* with its wild, unspoiled scenery and the picturesque stream of the same name running through it.

The gorge is approximately 2000 m. in length and its entrance is situated 2 kms. south of Koxarés.

From here we continue approximately 500 metres to the east and find ourselves at the 20.5 km. mark of the Rethymnon – Armenoi – Spili – Aghia Galini road. We take the opposite direction to that of route 14 (from south to north) and end up in Rethymnon.

Preveli Monastery, dating from the 16th or 17th century.

*Preveli, near the mouth
of the Kourtaliotis river.
One of the most idyllic spots
on the island.*

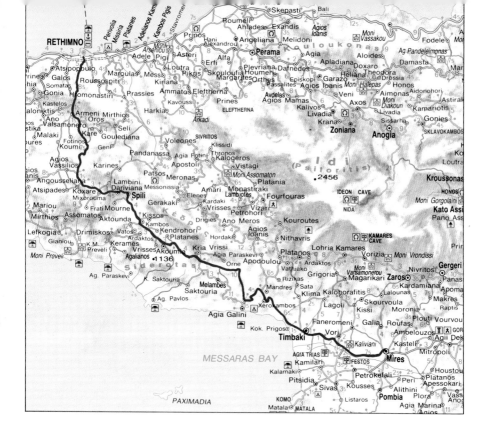

14

Rethymnon – Spili – Aghia Galini – Tymbaki – Voroi – Kalyviani monastery – Moires.

We leave Rethymnon and drive southwards until, at the 10th kilometre, we come to the village of *Armenoi,* where excavations have brought to light a large cemetery of the Late Minoan period. The graves contained clay sarcophagi decorated with paintings (Minoan religious symbols, hunting scenes etc.).

A great number of seal-stones were also found (Archaeological Museums of Rethymnon and Chania).

Just outside Armenoi, a fork to the left leads to Karé, Goulediana and Seli, while the main road continues south and 7.5 kms. later (19 kms. from Rethymnon) joins a side road leading westwards towards Aghios Vassilios, Aghios Ioannis and Sellia. A kilometre and a half after the intersection, another fork to the west leads to Koxarés, Asomato and the Preveli monastery (see route 13).

We continue along the main road for another 7.5 kms. towards the southeast and come to Spili (28 kms. from Rethymnon). This is a picturesque village built at an altitude of 430 metres, in verdant surroundings where sparkling springs, stone fountains, cool shady nooks and churches (Aghioi Theodori, Aghios Georgios, Metamorphosis tou Sotiros) with beautiful murals, create an idyllic picture. In the little square with the century–old plane trees, crystal clear water flows from a fountain, through the mouths of a whole row of carved lions' heads.

Left: Aghia Galini.
Above: The cool village of Spili with its abundant water.

We continue southwards towards Kambos Kissou, Akoumia and Kria Vryssi. (From Kambos a detour to the right leads to Aktounda, Vatos, Adraktos. Just outside Kria Vryssi there is also a detour to the right towards Melambes).

Our road ends up at *Aghia Galini* (54 kms. from Rethymnon, 78 kms. from Herakleion). This is a lovely seaside village in the sheltered Messara bay, built on a height above the picturesque little harbour, with an unlimited view towards the Libyan sea. It attracts many tourists and offers accommodation to suit every taste and pocket (hotels, pensions, rooms and flats to rent, camping sites etc.).

There are also many restaurants, tavernas, bars, discos, folk art shops etc.

On the eastern side of the bay, with its rocky shores, there are interesting marine caves which one can visit by boat. The Aghia Galini beach is a very popular one. Just beyond it there is a nudist beach.

To the west lie the wonderful beaches of Aghios Georgios and Aghios Pavlos, with their lovely sea. There are several restaurants and tavernas. One can also reach them by caïque. From Aghia Galini we turn northeastwards and, 6 kms. further along, near the village of

Mandres, the road turns southeastwards. It passes through Xerokambos and arrives at *Tymbaki* (13 kms. to the southeast of Aghia Galini).

Tymbaki is a large, prosperous village where early fruit and vegetables are grown, as well as citrus and olive trees. The village is plentifully supplied with water. The church of Saint Titus — the patron saint of Tymbaki — is worth a visit. It is built near an older church which was also dedicated to the same saint.

In 1822, the first important battle of Messara against the Turks took place in this village. The Greeks were victorious and seized several villages in the vicinity.

In 1941, the village was destroyed by the forces of occupation. At a distance of 1.5 kms. northwest of Tymbaki lies the seaside settlement of *Kokkinos Pyrgos* whose name, "red tower" comes from the mediaeval tower built with red earth which was a landmark of the place. The beach here is beautiful and the sea limpid.

Left: Aghia Galini, built amphitheatrically on a picturesque little harbour.
Top Right: Endless beaches at Aghia Galini.
Bottom Right: The beach of Aghios Pavlos

Four kilometres beyond Tymbaki, a road to the left leads to Voroi and Faneromeni.

The main road continues to the southeast.

We pass by the Kalyviani monastery which is built in a lovely green setting and is dedicated to the Holy Virgin.

The old church dates from the second Byzantine period.

During the independence struggle against the Turks, a new church was built which has three naves and a dome. It is dedicated to the Birthday of the Holy Virgin, the Annunciation and the Dormition of the Holy Virgin.

A small icon of the Annunciation — believed to perform miracles — was found in 1873 in the ruins of the old church and is kept in the new church.

Our route ends at *Moires* (25.5 kms. east of Aghia Galini and 77.5 from Rethymnon) (see route 6).

15

RETHYMNON - CHANIA

Rethymnon – Georgioupolis – Vrysses intersection – Fres – Vammos – Megala Chorafia – Aptera – Souda – Chania.

We take the new Rethymnon – Chania national road, and follow itinerary 13 until the flyover at the Georgioupolis–Vrysses intersection (26 kms. from Rethymnon). From this intersection one can choose to go to Vrysses, to *Fres* (a historic village which was in the forefront of the struggles against the Turks), *Vammos* (a pretty village whose inhabitants also were involved in the liberation struggles), Kefala, Kalamitsi, Exopolis, Georgioupolis. At the 41st kilometre along the national road, a flyover takes us to Kalyves – Plaka – Kokkino Chorio.

Another flyover, at the 44th km. also leads to Kalyves.

At the 46th km. there is a detour to the right, towards *Kalami.* At the 47th km. a detour to the left leads to *Megala Chorafia,* the site of *Ancient Aptera* and Stylos.

Aptera was a powerful commercial city which was built in the 7th century BC. Its ruins date from the pre–Hellenic, Hellenic and Roman periods. During the Byzantine period it continued to prosper. It was destroyed in 823 AD by the Saracens and, from that time on, it was never rebuilt or re–inhabited.

Above: The superb beach of Almyrida to the east of Kalyves.

During excavations on the site, a small temple of the early part of the 1st century BC was discovered, probably dedicated to Demeter and her daughter Kore. Statues, inscriptions, funerary steles, vessels, a headless statue of Hygeia (Archaeological Museum of Chania) were also among the finds. Its impressive Cyclopean walls and its immense vaulted cisterns are still well preserved. The ruins of a theatre have also survived.

The necropolis was situated to the west of the city. Rock–cut tombs of the Roman period were discovered, one of which contained clay Roman pots, oil lamps etc.

There is a monastery on the site dedicated to Saint John the Theologian.

A road at the 51st km. to the right takes us to *Souda,* 55 kms. from Rethymnon. Souda, the most important harbour of western Crete, and one of the safest in the Mediterranean, is built deep in the bay of the same name.

It has developed rapidly in recent years and has modern port installations and a naval base.

Today, the busy port of Souda is the main sea gate of western Crete. It is linked with Piraeus through frequent car–ferry services.

At the southern end of the bay, near Kalami, stands the Turkish fortress of *Idjeddin* which has been converted into a prison. Opposite the fortress, at the entrance to the bay, lies the *islet of Souda,* on which, between the years 1570–1573, the Venetians built a strong fortress, to protect the bay from pirate

Old engraving of Souda showing its strong Venetian fortress.

raids. The fortifications were so perfect that the Turks were unable to take the fortress and it remained in Venetian hands for half a century after Crete had fallen to the Turks. It was ceded to the Turks under the Treaty of 1715.

The Venetians had provided the fortress with a great number of cannon and abundant ammunition, while its walls encircled the entire islet. Within the enclosure were barracks, the residence of the "Provleptis", reservoirs, ammunition depots, even a loggia. Today, very little remains of this grand Venetian castle, and even those few ruins which can still be seen, do not belong to the original fortress, but to the restorations effected later by the Turks when it came into their hands.

We continue along the secondary coastal road and 6.5 kms. further along arrive at *Chania*.

CHANIA

This is the largest and most important town of western Crete, with a population of over 60,000 inhabitants.

It is situated on the eastern shore of the bay of Chania, and is built on the neck of the peninsula, on the site of ancient Kydonia.

It is the administrative, commercial, economic and communications centre of the prefecture of the same name, of which it is the capital.

It is linked with Piraeus by the boats running from Souda harbour, to and from which there is a regular bus service.

It has an airport near Sternes at Akrotiri, 15 kms. east of the town. There are very frequent flights to Athens in the summer, less frequent in the winter. Olympic Airways coaches, KTEL buses and taxis convey passengers to and from the airport.

History

The excavations in the Kastelli quarter proved that present–day Chania was built on the the site of ancient Kydonia. Many graves and a rich collection of pottery of various periods, grave offerings of the Mycenean period, a structure in the style of a Minoan palace, parts of frescoes of the Late Minoan period, a fragment of a stirrup jar with an inscription in Linear B, three clay tablets in Linear B script, statues of the Roman period, a magnificent mosaic of the late Hellenistic period, were all discovered here. These rich finds confirm that in the area of the present–day town, an important settlement had been established since Neolithic times, which developed through the centuries to become Kydonia in later years.

Kydonia was a large city which flourished during the Roman period, and even boasted a theatre.

We see the city mentioned under the name of Kydonia until the end of the 1st Byzantine period, at which time it was a bishop's see. It is believed to have been destroyed by the Saracens in 828 AD. Remains of the Roman theatre have not been preserved, since, as foreign travellers of the time record, the Venetians demolished it to use the ma-

terials for the construction of the city walls.

During the 2nd Byzantine period, Chania lost its prestige, no longer holding the status of an important town, but only that of an unimportant village.

When the Venetians settled at Kastelli, they fortified the town, built the palace of the "Retturis" within the fortress, and also the Roman Catholic cathedral and the houses of the Venetian officials. At the foot of the hill, they established the "Burghi", which were later encircled by newer walls. The new walls were built between 1336 and 1356, but these, too, were not strong enough so, almost two hundred years later, in 1536, the famous Italian civil engineer Michele Sanmicheli came to the town to design the more recent walls.

However, the new fortifications were still insufficient. In 1536, new additions were made and the construction was completed in 1568.

In 1645, after a siege of two months, the Turks took the fort and occupied the town.

Later they repaired and fortified the destroyed portions of the walls, ruins of which still survived up to the early years of our century.

They fell into ruin partly owing to their age, but chiefly because the inhabitants themselves demolished them to build new structures on top, using the materials from the walls themselves. Thus, today, only very few remains have been preserved.

In 1851, the Turks transferred the seat of the Ottoman administration of Crete to Chaniá.

In 1897, after the island was declared an autonomous republic, the Turks withdrew and Chania became the capital of the Cretan State and the seat of the High Commissioner.

In 1913, together with the rest of Crete, Chania was incorporated into the free Greek State. During the heroic Battle of Crete, in May 1941, the area of Chania became a theatre of operations.

During the difficult years of the German occupation, the inhabitants of Chania were actively involved in the resistance.

Tour of the town

Chania has, to a large degree, retained its local colour. It is one of the loveliest towns in Greece and the many vestiges of its past give it a particular charm. Entire Venetian, Turkish and Jewish neighbourhoods still survive, with well–preserved buildings, while the modern town, continuing to develop, is built according to well–designed plans, with parks and attractive edifices. It differs considerably from the tasteless big towns of today.

Chania disposes of a large number of beds in hotels of various categories. There are also pensions and guest houses. There are many restaurants — some of them offering foreign specialities — tavernas, seafood restaurants, "ouzeries", pastry shops, coffee shops, pubs etc. in every neighbourhood and especially in the harbour area, which is lit up by the shop lights in the evenings and sparkles like a fairy–tale town.

One can enjoy oneself in the discos, or one might prefer to listen to Cretan music.

There are cinemas, theatres and concerts, exhibitions, lectures and a variety of cultural activities.

Generally, Chania is a town which caters for all tastes and interests.

We shall begin our tour of the town from the old quarters.

Topanas is the western aristocratic neighbourhood of old Chania, which got its name from the "topia" or cannon which the Turks had set up on the ramparts of San Salvatore. During the later years of Ottoman rule, this neighbourhood was inhabited by wealthy Christian families, and here were situated the Consulates of the Great Powers, before they moved to Halepa. Quite a few Venetian buildings, in the narrow picturesque streets around the harbour, are still standing. At the entrance to the harbour, at the northernmost point of the quarter, we find the "Firkas" fortress (the word means military unit), which was built in 1629. The Chania Naval Museum is housed here today, as well as a summer theatre. It is closely bound to the history of the town. This is where the Greek flag was first hoisted on December 1st, 1913, during an official ceremony celebrating the union of Crete with Greece.

Opposite the Firkas fortress stand a 16th century Venetian lighthouse,

which was restored to its present form by the Egyptians in the mid–18th century. The harbour, sheltered from the north wind and sea by strong breakwaters, lies to the east of the Topanas quarter.

The Jewish quarter ("Ovriaki"), is situated to the south of Topanas. The most important edifice of this neighbourhood is the imposing Venetian church of Saint Francis, which used to belong to the Franciscan monks and which today houses the Chania Archaeological Museum.

The Turks had turned this church into a mosque ("Yiousouf Pasha Djami"), adding new structures and a small minaret which was destroyed during World War II. To the south of the Jewish quarter is the Schiavo or Lando bastion and a portion of the town walls.

The Sandrivani quarter (Eleftherios Venizelos square). This was the heart of old Chania. It dates from the Venetian period, but we do not know the name it bore at that time. It owes its present name to a Turkish fountain (syndrivani) which stood in the middle of the square.

Further north is the Hassan Pacha mosque — built by the Arabs — which houses the Information Office of the Municipality of Chania. Next to it we find the Port Authority kiosk, where the old Customs House once stood.

The Kastelli quarter. This quarter lies to the east of the harbour. Here, as the archaeological finds indicate, was the site of ancient Kydonia. The Venetians settled in this area in 1252. They built walls and, within the enclosure, on the highest point of the hill, they erected the "Rettore's" Palazzo. During the Turkish occupation, this was where the Pasha resided.

Further south stood the Venetian Cathedral, which the Turks turned into a mosque when they took the fortress.

During the later years of the Turkish occupation, several wealthy families of Chania lived in the Kastelli neighbourhood.

Today, nothing remains of the buildings except the base of the northern side of the walls.

The Splantza or Plaza quarter. This was the Turkish quarter. It lies to the east of the Kastelli quarter, near the harbour with its shipyards which were built by the Venetians in the late 15th century. Today, only nine out of the

Picturesque views of Chania.

twenty arches of the shipyards are preserved.

In the square stands the church of Saint Nicholas.

Also worthy of notice is the small Venetian church of Saint Rocco with a Latin inscription of 1630, and the Greek Orthodox Church of Aghioi Anargyroi.

Other characteristic spots in the town of Chania are: The impressive *Municipal Market,* in the centre of town (1897 Square), which was built in 1911.

The restored 1645 mosque, in the harbour, where the offices of the Greek Tourism Organization are housed.

The *Turkish Baths:* this is a building with a characteristic dome, in the harbour area.

The *Venetian Palace* in Zambelli street, with a heraldic emblem and a Latin inscription.

The *Renieri Gate* in Theophanous Street.

The *Cathedral of Chania* ("Trimartyri") in a square east of Chalidon Street. This church has three naves, dedicated to the Presentation of the Holy Virgin, to Saint Nicholas and to the Three Hierarchs, respectively.

A visit to the *Chania Municipal Gardens* is also worthwhile. This is the Turkish "baktshé", which was designed in 1870, following European models, by Reouf Pacha.

The most important among the newer neighbourhoods of Chania are: The historic *Halepa quarter,* where the palace of the High Commissioner, the house of Eleftherios Venizelos and the Church of Saint Magdalene, built in the Russo—Byzantine style, are to be found; the *Kainouria Chora* (New Town) to the west; the *Koum Kapi,* outside the walls on the eastern side, and the *Bolari* quarter, to the east of Koum Kapi.

MUSEUMS

Archaeological Museum of Chania
(21 Chalidon street, in the church of Saint Francis, tel. no.0821/20.334).

It contains important finds from the excavations in the Chania region and the whole of western Crete, dating from the Neolithic to the Roman period. The most important exhibits are:

Vases and weapons from the Minoan necropolis, tablets in Linear A script and a fragment of an amphora with inscriptions in Linear B. Impressive polychrome sarcophagi and the sarcophagus of the sacred hunt from the Armenoi cemetery.

A collection of Early Geometric and Geometric pottery, Hellenistic statues from the Lissos Asclepieion.

Mosaics from Chania depicting Poseidon and Amymone, Dionysus and Arjadne. Classical and Hellenistic figurines, a collection of coins of various periods, glass vessels of Greco–Roman times from Tarra and many other interesting exhibitis.

Historical Archives of Crete and Museum.
It is housed in a neo-classical building, at 20, Sfakianaki Street, tel. 22.606. It includes historic documents, collections, archives, religious vessels, maps, coins, a photographic collection, etc.

In a special room dedicated to Eleftherios Venizelos are exhibited personal objects and mementos belonging to the great Greek statesman. An important library and a folk art collection are also housed here.

Chania Naval Museum:
It is housed in a building of the "Firkas" fortress, (tel. no. 26.437). Here are exhibited models of ships from antiquity to modern times and relics from the historic battles of the Greek Navy.

Municipal Library:
This is housed in a room of the Municipal building on Kydonias Avenue, tel. no. 23.273.

In includes 60,000 volumes of books, 15,000 magazines and newspapers, and the personal library of Eleftherios Venizelos comprising 8,500 volumes.

Glass perfume bottles in Phoenician style (late 4th century BC). Archaeological Museum of Chania. (above).
Clay tablet depicting the god Apollo in relief. (Archaeological Museum of Chania). (below).

eft: Poseidon and Amymone, from the
osaic floor of a Roman house of the 3rd
ntury AD in Chania. (Archaeological
useum of Chania).
ight: Central design from the mosaic floor of
e "Dionysus house" (3rd century AD):
ionysus discovers Ariadne on the island of
axos. (Archaeological Museum of Chania).

STARTING FROM CHANIA

Chania – Chryssopighi monastery – Mourniés – Therissos – return. Chania – Akrotiri – Aghia Triada monastery – Gouvernetto monastery.

We start off from Chania and drive south-eastwards towards Souda. At the third kilometre, we meet a detour to the right leading to the *Monastery of Chryssopighi* or *Zoödochos Pighi*.

This monastery was founded by the Chartofylakas family of Chania, around 1600. On the gate is an inscription and under it the coat of arms of the founder's family, with the date 1863, at which time it was probably renovated.

The monastery is surrounded by a wall. In the centre of the precinct stands the church, with three conchae and three domes, dedicated to the Life–giving Fountain, "Zoödochos Pighi". Important documents are kept in the monastery.

From Chryssopighi we can continue westwards towards *Mourniés* or return by the same road to Chania and, from there, drive southwards, in which case, 3.5 kms. further along, we come to the verdant village of Mourniés, the birth-place of Eleftherios Venizelos.

The statesman's house is still standing, and contains several of his personal belongings.

Not far from the village, is situated the *Monastery of Aghios Eleftherios*. This is a dependency of the Chryssopighi monastery and dates from the 17th century.

Nearby, there is a small church dedicated to the Prophet Elijah, with a decora-

tion in relief and inscriptions dating from 1578. Another road, almost parallel to the Mourniés road, also starts from Chania and leads southwards. It passes through the village of Perivolia and ends up in the heroic village of *Therissos* (16 kms. south of Chania).

Part of the route passes through the 6 km. long Therissos gorge or Venizelos gorge, as it is also called.

The inhabitants of the village took part in the struggle for independence against the Turkish occupation. However, the most important event in its history is more recent. It was from this small village that, in 1905, Eleftherios Venizelos issued his call for a revolution against the regime of Prince George of Greece, who had been set up as High Commissioner of the autonomous "Cretan Republic" by the European Powers. This uprising, which has gone down in history as the Revolution of Therissos, was quashed by the Great Powers, but as a result of it, Prince George resigned, a year later.

In the village, we can still see the building which served as Venizelos' headquarters.

Two and a half kilometres north of Therissos is situated the cave of *Kato Sarakina* or *Elliniko*. The potsherds found here testify to this cave having been a place of worship.

We now return to Chania, from where our next tour, to the Akrotiri peninsula, starts.

We take the road leading to the airport, in an easterly direction. After four and a half kilometres, we turn left and as-

Entrance to the monastery of Aghia Triada ton Tzangarolon.

Mournies, the house of Eleftherios Venizelos.

*The grave of Eleftherios Venizelos
on the hill of Profitis Ilias (Akrotiri).*

cend the hill of Profitis Ilias, where there is a simple memorial and the tombs of Eleftherios Venizelos and his son, Sophocles. From this hill we can enjoy a superb panoramic view of Chania and its vast expanse of beach.

The road continues eastwards towards Korakiés and Aroni, picturesque villages with houses in traditional local style. Just beyond Aroni there is a detour to the north (while the road to the airport continues eastwards) which leads to the *Aghia Triada ton Tzangarolon* Monastery (15.5 kms. from Chania), near the village of Koumares, in a beautiful natural setting. In the middle of the monastery precinct stands the church of Aghia Triada — the Holy Trinity. This is a cruciform, domed church with two side chapels, one of which is dedicated to the Zoödochos Pighi and the other to Saint John the Theologian. The facade of the church is impressive. There are two large Doric–style columns and one smaller, Corinthian–style column on either side of the main entrance. The facade also bears an inscription in Greek

The church of Aghia Triada, a cruciform church with a dome and an impressive facade.

Marathi beach on Akrotiri, to the east of the airport.

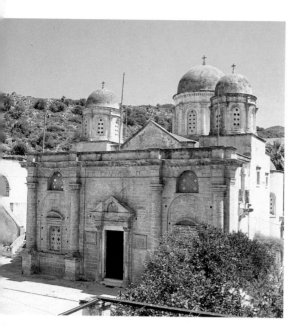

and the date 1631.

Above the monastery's cellar door there is an older date — 1613. The belfry was built much later, in 1864. This monastery played an important part in the insurrections against the Turks and, when it was destroyed, it was rebuilt again by the monks. It was very wealthy. In 1833, a boarding school was established here while, in 1892, a seminary was set up, which numbered among its teachers many eminent scholars.

The monastery also has a library with rare books and old codices, as well as icons worthy of mention, painted by Mercurius of Santorini, a well–known religious painter of his time.

Four kilometres to the north (half of the road is a dirt road), we find the *Gouvernetto Monastery,* surrounded by a fortress–like enclosure in the shape of a quadrangle, with four square towers at its corners.

There are fifty cells, some of which are vaulted. In the centre of the enclosure stands the church of the Presentation of the Holy Virgin, also known as Lady of the Angels.

Its facade shows a strong Italianate influence in its sculptured decoration, columns etc.

There are two side chapels, one of which is dedicated to Saint John the Hermit or the Stranger (Aghios Ioannis o Xenos), and the other to the Aghioi Deka.

Close by, to the north of the Gouvernetto monastery, in a wild ravine — the Avlaki ravine — we find the *Monastery of Saint John the Hermit or the Stranger,* better known as the *Katholikon.*

The little church is entirely cut out of the rock and only its western side is built. Around the courtyard are the cells. To the left of the church is the entrance to the cave where the founder of the monastery, Saint John the Hermit, lived and died. It is the bed of an old underground river. Its length is 135 metres, its entire area approximately 1500 sq. metres, and it has a rich decoration of stalactites and stalagmites. Near the entrance to the cave there is a basin with water which the faithful believe to be holy water.

On the western coast of the Akrotiri peninsula is the seaside settlement of *Kalathas* with its beautiful beach and tourist accommodations.

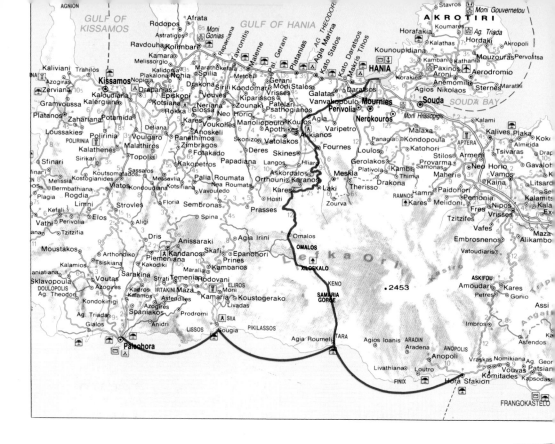

17

OMALOS – SAMARIA GORGE

Chania – Alikianos – Fournes – Lakkoi – Omalos – Xyloskalo – Samaria gorge – Aghia Roumeli. Return through Chora Sfakion, or Soughia, or Palaeochora.

We leave Chania and drive southwards, passing through the settlement of Vamvakopoulo (3.4 kms.) and then *Aghiá* (9.5 kms.), a village with many flowing springs.

On our journey southwards we pass through the verdant valley of Keritis, with its rich groves of citrus trees.

At the 12th km. point, a fork to the right takes us, after approximately 500 m., to *Alikianos.*

Before the turn–off to Alikianos, the road branches out, the left fork leading southwards to Skiniés – Nea Roumata – Prasses – Aghia Irene (Aghia Irene gorge) – Epanochori – Rodovani – Moni, and ending up at Soughia (70 kms. from Chania). The other fork to the left leads to Omalos and the Samaria gorge, which is our destination.

Alikianos was the fief of the Venetian family of Da Molin. Here was situated their imposing castle, of which only scant remains can still be seen. Not far away was found a carving in relief of the family's coat of arms.

The inhabitants of Alikianos put up a strong resistance against the Turks, as they did, in more recent times, against the German forces of occupation. The Germans retaliated by executing the rebellious patriots and, after the liberation, a modest monument was set up to commemorate their sacrifice.

A Byzantine church of Saint George, built in 1243, with very interesting murals, still stands.

At the 15th kilometre of the main route, we meet the village of *Fournes.* From here, the road branches out, one branch leading to the village of *Meskla* (6 kms.), where there are two churches with frescoes worth seeing.

We will follow the right branch and, after climbing a road with many curves for 9.5 kms., on the northwestern flank of the White Mountains, we come to *Lakkoi,* a lovely village amid olive trees and vineyards, built on the mountainside, with a wonderful view of the snow–capped peaks.

The inhabitants of Lakkoi took an active part in the liberation struggles against the Turks.

The road continues westwards, towards Karés, and then turns south again. We continue to climb. We pass through the historic "Strata" of the Moussouros family, which was celebrated in the old "rizitika" songs, and arrive at the highest point of our route (1200 m.) from where there is a panoramic view of the *Omalos plateau,* with its surrounding ring of imposing mountain peaks.

The plateau is in the shape of an irregular circle, approximately 4 kilometres in diameter. Almost in the centre of it lies the small settlement of *Omalos* (39 kms. from Chania). As a result of its

223

Above. The wild beauty of the Omalos plateau.
Right. The impressive Samaria gorge.

inaccessibility and its naturally fortified position, the area served as a base of operations and a refuge for revolutionary fighters many times during the island's history.

Our road passes through the plateau and, after four kilometres, ends up at the *Xyloskalo* ("wooden stairway") ridge (altitude: 1,227 m.), 43 kms. south of Chania, where the entrance to the gorge is situated. On this spot there was once a wooden stairway to facilitate the descent, which is how the place got its name. A small guest house operates here, and the view from it over the surrounding area is superb.

Just before Xyroskalo, a little road leads to the Skiing Centre of *Kallerghi*, at an altitude of 1680 m.

Those visitors who have decided to walk through the gorge, begin their descent from Xyloskalo, down some steps to begin with and then along a footpath. The sites called "Portes" ("doors") are extremely impressive, as here the walls of the ravine almost touch each other (3-4 m.). The narrowest "porta" is the one near the exit to Aghia Roumeli. A little stream, which becomes a raging river in the winter, flows down the middle of the gorge.

The gorge has been declared a National Park in order to protect its rare flora and fauna, and in particular the Cretan mountain goat, called "kri-kri" or the "wild one" by the locals. In 1980, Samaria was awarded a prize by the Council of Europe, as one of the most beautiful virgin sites in Europe.

The descend into the gorge is quite difficult and crossing it takes about 6-8 hours. Hikers must wear sturdy walking shoes and hats, and carry along with them only the essentials. These do not include water, as there are springs along the way. One is allowed through the gorge from the beginning of May to the end of October. During the rest of the year, the melting snows on the high walls of the gorge and the rains raise the level of the innocent stream and turn it into a dangerous torrent. The best time of the year for the hike is May or the end of September – beginning of October, when it is not too hot, although it is relatively cool inside the gorge, since the sun only reaches down into it at noon, when its rays fall perpendicularly between the sheer walls.

The taking of photographs is permitted, but the following are not allowed:
– spending the night inside the gorge
– lighting a fire or smoking
– hunting or fishing
– swimming
– cutting plants, flowers or branches
– any kind of noise
– the destruction of birds' nests or eggs
– pets
– fouling the area
– drinking alcoholic beverages.

Near the entrance to the gorge is the chapel of Saint Nicholas, surrounded by trees and springs from which flows deliciously cool water. It is believed that this was the site of an ancient temple to Apollo, and that the ancient town of Kaino lay close by.

Half–way through the gorge lies the old settlement of *Samaria,* where a few families of woodcutters used to live. It was abandoned a few years after the gorge was declared a National Park (1962). Here is a small Byzantine church of Saint Mary the Egyptian. The name "Samaria" comes from a corrupt form of the name of the church: Ossia Maria – Siamaria – Samaria.

A telephone has been installed in the abandoned settlement, as well as a police station, a chemist's shop and a heliport. Two mules are also stationed here for use in cases of emergency. At four points along the trail, a first aid box and fire extinguishers have been installed, as well as other tools to help put out fires. Crossing the gorge, also called the "Farangas" by the locals, is a unique and unforgettable experience. Hikers are face to face with nature and its wild beauty. Their difficult hike along the rugged, downward path is rewarded by the impressive, pristine scenery, untouched by human hands and immensely beautiful, which leaves them with a feeling of awe and infinite admiration for the pure and unalloyed grandeur around them.

As they come out of the gorge, dazzled by its beauty and tired after the long trek, the hikers are faced with another picturesque scene: a group of mules and their muleteers, waiting to take those who wish to ride, for a small fee, to *Aghia Roumeli.*

This is a seaside settlement with a wonderful beach and a lovely limpid sea, about 1.5 kms. from the exit of the gorge. It is built on the site of the ancient city of Tarra. In the summer, the village is very busy, since all the visitors to the gorge end up here, but also because of the many summer residents who choose Aghia Roumeli for its incomparable beaches.

There are a few beds in a small hotel and a guest–house and there are also rooms to rent. In the summer months there are restaurants, tavernas and discos.

The village is cut off on the landward side. It is connected only by sea — small boats make regular journeys — with Chora Sfakion to the east, with Soughia and Palaeochora to the west and from there by KTEL buses with Chania and Rethymnon.

All the tourist agencies organise excursions to the Samaria gorge.

Information on the KTEL services to Xyloskalo (for the outward journey) and from Chora Sfakia (for the return journey) can be obtained from the Information Offices of the Municipality of Chania and from the offices of the Greek Tourism Organization in Rethymnon, Chania and Herakleion.

It is preferable to take a KTEL bus or a coach for this journey. Private cars are not a good option since they would have to be left at the entrance to the gorge, at Xyloskalo.

Aghia Roumeli. Stone chapel. (right).
The beach of Aghia Roumeli, where the Samaria gorge ends. (below).

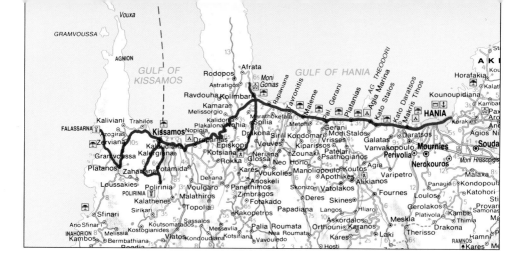

18

Chania – Maleme – Tavronites – Kolymbari – Gonia Monastery – (Spilia – Cracona – Episkopi) – Kissamos – Polyrrhenia – Platanos – Falasarna.

Starting out from Chania we drive westwards towards Kissamos, along the coast. At the 4th km. we come to the site called Makris Tichos ("Long Wall"), where there is a road for Daratsos and *Galatas,* the scene of an important battle against the Germans. Further along the main road we meet lovely seaside villages and settlements: Kato Daratsos, Kato Stalos, Aghia Marina, Platanias (the islet of Aghioi Theodoroi lies opposite), Palaeo Gerani, *Maleme* (16.5 kms. west of Chania), all of which provide accommodation for visitors, tavernas, restaurants, etc. Southbound roads from almost all of these villages lead us to densely–wooded areas.

Maleme was where the old airport of Chania, which has now been abandoned, was situated. This is also where the massive German invasion by parachutists began, during the Battle of Crete. North of the village, at a place called Kafkalos, a vaulted late Minoan tomb, which had been plundered and only contained some potsherds and two sealstones, was discovered.

Maleme today is a modern tourist village providing accommodation for visitors. One kilometre from Maleme is the German military cemetery. At the 20th km. lies the village of *Tavronitis* which got its name from the river of the same name. A road from this village leads southwards to Palaeochora (see routes 17 and 19).

Left: The beach of Aghioi Apostoloi.

Top: Kolymbari and Gonia Monastery.

We continue westwards, and after Rapaniana, 23 kms. along this road — the main road continues southwestwards towards Kissamos — we come to an intersection. The road northwards leads to Kolymbari and the Gonia monastery.

Kolymbari is a lovely seaside village attracting many tourists. It is built on the westernmost point of the Bay of Chania. To the north lies the peninsula of Rhodopos.

One kilometre north of Kolymbari is the *Monastery of Gonia,* dedicated to the Holy Virgin Hodegetria (who guides). It is surrounded by a courtyard, around which are built the monks' cells, the abbot's quarters, the refectory, the storerooms and cellars. Only a few books survived the fire set by the Turks in 1866 to the rich library of the monastery. There is also a collection of important post–Byzantine icons and a treasury containing holy relics and other precious objects.

During the Greek War of Independence of 1812, it served as a hospital and, during the German occupation, it was the focus of an active resistance movement. To the north of the monastery stands the building of the *Orthodox Academy of Crete* and 2 kilometres

229

further on, the modest *monument erected in memory of the Military Cadets* who fell during the Battle of Crete.

We return to the 23rd km. of the main Chania – Kissamos road and take the road southwards to *Spilia*. On a wooded hill stands a church dedicated to the Holy Virgin, the walls of which are covered with murals. We then come to *Drakonas* and *Episkopi* (3 kms. southwest of Draconas). At Episkopi, it is worth visiting the impressive *Rotonda*, a church dedicated to the Archangel Michael, the architectural style of which is unique in Crete.

We continue along the main road. Outside Kolymbari, 2.5 kms. after the intersection, we come to a right turn–off leading to *Rhodopos*, in the heart of the peninsula of the same name.

We continue further west and, after passing through various villages: Kaledonia, Plakalona, Drapanias, Kaloudiana, we come to *Kissamos* or *Kastelli*, 32 kms. west of Chania. From Kaloudiana, a road southwards takes one to Topolia – Chrysoskalitissa — Palaeochora (route 19).

Kissamos is a small town built on a bay of the same name, on the site of ancient Kissamos, which was the harbour of neighbouring Polyrrhenia.

The town stretches alongside a wonderful sandy beach, at the edge of a verdant plain planted with olive groves and vineyards.

The ruins that we can see today date mainly from the Roman period, when the town was particularly prosperous.

The Venetians built a fort — Castello — here, which gave the town its name. The fort was destroyed by Barbarossa and, in 1646, it was taken by the Turks. The ruins, which are visible today, are additions and repairs made by its latest conquerors. From Kissamos there are regular services to Gytheion, on the mainland of the Peloponnese, and the island of Kythera.

Left above: The beach of Aghia Marina.
Left below: Platanias.

Below: Kastelli (Kissamos).

Seven kilometres to the south lie the ruins of the ancient city of *Polyrrhenia*. It was built on a naturally fortified hill, not very far from the present–day settlement of the same name. It was an important city of western Crete, with a strong acropolis and, as the finds indicate, it was inhabited from the Archaic to the Roman period. It was re-inhabited in the 10th century. It had an impressive aqueduct, ruins of which are still preserved.

We continue a little further west of Kissamos. The road leaves the coast and turns south towards Zerviana, Gramvousa and *Platanos* (10 kms. from Kissamos). Outside the village of Platanos, there is a road to the right, only half of which is tarred, leading north to *Ancient Falasarna* (5.5 kms. from Platanos) on the northwestern coast of the island.

In ancient times, this was an important commercial and naval centre, built on a naturally fortified position and serving as a harbour for neighbouring Polyrrhenia.

The beach of Falasarna, with its fine sand and lovely coves, is one of the most beautiful in Crete.

In this modern settlement one can find rooms to rent and tavernas. To the north lies the deserted peninsula which ends up at the Vouza point. Opposite the cape is the small desert island of Agria ("wild") Gramvousa and further south that of Imeri ("mild, tame") Gramvousa or plain *Gramvousa*. The Venetians built a fortress on the latter islet, on a sheer rock; it was taken by the Cretan insurgents in 1825, and was used by them as their base for suprise assaults against the Turks.

Gramvousa was the first portion of Cretan territory to become free. In 1828 it fell into the hands of the British and the French.

Right: The Castle of Gramvousa,
built by the Venetians on a sheer rock.

Below: The beach of Falasarna.

19

Kissamos – Kaloudiana – Topolia (Topolia ravine – Aghia Sophia cave) – Myloi – (Elos – Kefali – Chrysoskalitissa Monastery) – Strovles – Plemeniana – Palaeochora.
Return: Palaeochora – Plemeniana – Kantanos (Anisaraki – Rodovani – Elyros – Soughia) – Floria – Kakopetro – Voukolies – Tavronitis.

From Kissamos we continue eastwards along the main Chania – Kissamos road and, at the 4th kilometre, at the village of *Kaloudiana* (see route 18), we turn right and follow a right fork to the south. The route is enchanting. We pass through the picturesque villages of Potamida and Voulgaro and find ourselves at *Topolia* (8 kms. from the intersection), a traditional village with flowing streams, built amphitheatrically on a wooded hill. Here begins the Topoliana ravine, which is approximately 1500 m. in length. Its walls are high (300 m.) and sheer, and the scenery is luxuriant. To the right passes the road for Palaeochora, and at this point the road forms a tunnel.

On the right side of the road is the cave of *Aghia Sophia* with its small church of the same name. The cave has stalactites and stalagmites and is interesting archaeologically because of the fragments of pottery of the Neolithic period which were found here. Its exit is near the village of Kartsomatados.

We continue southwards for *Myloi*. Outside the village, there is a bifurcation. We can visit the convent of Chryso-

skalitissa, if we take the right fork towards Elos and *Kefali* – where there is a church dedicated to the Transfiguration of Christ, with frescoes dating from 1300. Outside Kefali, we find a dirt road (11 kms.) which, after passing through the villages of Vathi and Plokamiana, leads us to the Chrysoskalitissa convent, on the southwestern coast of Crete (72 kms. southwest of Chania). The convent is built on a rock, on the site of an old monastic community, and has a superb view. Its church has two naves, dedicated to the Dormition of the Holy Virgin and to the Holy Trinity respectively.

In the small settlement of the same name, there are a few rooms to rent.

Five kilometres further south (along the same dirt road), we can see the islet of *Elafonissi*, to the west of the coast, from which it is separated by a shallow stretch of sea of about 100 m. in width and not deeper than 0.80 m.

The beaches and the sea in this area are glorious, but near the convent the shores are rocky and steep.

From the intersection at Myloi we follow the left fork, in a southeasterly direction and, two kilometres further along, we come to the village of *Strovles*, in a beautiful natural setting with bubbling streams and many chestnut trees.

The convent of Chrysoskalitissa
Pp. 236-237: Elafonissi.

235

Above: Palaeochora, the picturesque town.
Right: Views from Palaeochora.

We continue for another 8 kilometres (this is mostly a dirt road) and arrive at *Plemeniana*, where there is a church dedicated to Saint George, decorated with murals which are worth seeing.

At this point we meet the road which starts from Tavronitis (see route 18) and takes a southerly direction towards Palaeochora, passing through the western part of the island from north to south. We follow this road southwards and pass through the villages of Kakodiki, Vlithias, Kalamos (in this region there are interesting Byzantine churches with 13th century frescoes), to end up at *Palaeochora* (74.5 kms. southwest of Chania, 55 kms. from Tavronitis).

The picturesque small town on the Libyan sea has developed into an important tourist centre, with many places to stay, tavernas, restaurants, discos, bars, etc. In the summer it attracts many visitors, as well as the hikers who come down from the Samaria gorge to Aghia Roumeli and then take the little boats to Palaeochora (see route 17).

Small boats also link Palaeochora to Soughia and Chora Sfakion to the east, and to the islet of Gavdos in the Libyan sea.

Tourist agencies operating in the town organize excursions to the Samaria gorge from here.

In 1282, the duke of Crete, Marino Gradonico, built a fortress here which he called Selino — perhaps from the name of the area — as a protection against Cretan insurgents.

The fortress then gave its name to the entire province, which is called the province of Selino.

The insurgents destroyed the fortress, the Venetians rebuilt it and developed a "burgo", a settlement, around it.

In 1539 it was taken by Barbarossa and in 1653 it fell into the hands of the Turks, who repaired extensive parts of the destroyed walls.

The fortress, which is very similar to the Mirabello and Ierapetra fortresses, has three towers, officials' quarters, barracks, a church, a reservoir, etc.

Today, one can see ruins which clearly show the marks of the repairs and additions made by the Turks.

Below the fortress lies the old neighbourhood with its narrow alleys.

To the west of the village is situated the lovely beach of *Pacheia Ammos,* one of the most popular in the region.

From Palaeochora, we begin our return to Tavronitis. Following the same road (now in a northerly direction), we arrive at Plemeniana. From there we continue northeastwards towards *Kantanos* (2.5 kms. from Plemeniana), in the fertile valley of Selino, with its olive groves, chestnut trees and vineyards. The pretty village was razed to the ground on June 3rd, 1941, by the occupying forces, and many of its inhabitants were executed in reprisal for the murder of German soldiers by resistance fighters from Kantanos.

In the region there are many interesting Byzantine churches. From Kantanos, a road — in rather poor condition — forking out to the right of the main road, leads in an easterly–southeasterly direction, passing through the villages of Anisaraki, Te-

menia, Rodovani, and comes to the little seaside village of *Soughia* (see route 17).

To the west of the village is the site of the coastal Doric village of *Lissos,* which flouriched mainly during the Roman and Byzantine periods.

It was well–known throughout Crete for its mineral springs and an important Asclepieion. Many statues were found on the site — some of them life–size, many of them headless — and important votive offerings, among which a little gold snake (Archaeological Museum of Chania).

Lissos also knew a period of prosperity during Byzantine times, as is evidenced by the ruins of two early Christian basilicas which were discovered here.

The Doric city of *Elyros,* an autonomous city, flourished during the Roman and early Byzantine period, and was situated about 500 m. east of the village of Rodovani. Here, a statue of a man was found. From his stance, he has been named the "philosopher" (Archaeological Museum of Chania).

From Kantanos we continue along our main route northwards to Floria, situated at the highest spot of the road (at an altitude of 570 m.), and Kakopetro. At this point there is a fork to the right, leading southeastwards to Palia Roumata.

We continue northwards towards *Voukoliés* and after 8 kms. arrive at Tavronitis (53 kms. from Palaeochora), which is the end of our journey.

From there we can either drive eastwards towards Chania (20 kms.) or westwards towards Kissamos (22.5 kms.).

Soughia beach.

240

USEFUL INFORMATION
PREFECTURE OF HERAKLION

How to get there

By car–ferry from Piraeus: There are daily services (more frequent in the summer and less so in the winter). The distance is 174 nautical miles and the trip takes approximately 12 hours.

There are also other boats of the "barren line" linking Herakleion to Piraeus and the islands of Santorini, Ios, Karpathos, Naxos, Paros, Rhodes and Anafi.

By car-ferry from Thessaloniki: There is a year–round service which starts from Thessaloniki and calls at the islands of Tinos, Mykonos, Paros, Santorini. In the summer the itinerary also includes the islands of Skiathos, Syros and Ios.

During the summer months there is a daily local service by boat from Herakleion to Santorini.

By air from Athens: Frequent daily flights link Herakleion to Athens in the summer; these become less frequent in the winter. The flight takes approximately 50 mins. and the Herakleion Airport is 4.8 kms. of the town to the east, passengers can use the urban buses, Olympic Airways coaches and taxis for the journey to and from the airport.

By air from Thessaloniki: There are two flights a week. The flight takes 1 hr. 15 mins. There is also a flight from Herakleion to *Rhodes* (throughout the year), and to *Mykonos, Paros* and *Santorini* (only int he summer months).

Charter flights: frequent charter flights daily link Herakleion Airport to many European cities. These flights decrease in frequency in the winter.

By road. The road network is generally good and there are frequent bus services, both local and regional. There are regular bus connections with the airport, the suburbs, and with almost all the villages in the prefecture as well as with Aghios Nikolaos, Siteia, Ierapetra, Rethymnon and Chania.

Car and motorcycle rentals. Taxis.
At Herakleion, at Herakleion Airport and in many villages there are agencies where one can hire cars and motorcycles. There are also many taxis available.

Tourist Agencies. These are plentiful in the town itself and also in other places frequented by tourists. They organize outings and excursion throughout the island.

Entertainment-Sports-Leisure activities

In Herakleion there are many restaurants, tavernas, seafood tavernas, ouzo bars, pizza parlours, and restaurants offering foreign cuisine, tavernas with local specialities etc.

There are also bars, cafeterias, pastry – shops, discos, cinemas, cafe-theatres, places where one can enjoy Cretan music, songs and dances.

In most villages there are small tavernas, where one can find a simple meal as well as local specialities. In places which are frequented by tourists one can find all sorts of restaurants and entertainment.

On the northern coast, good beaches for *swimming* are: the organized beach of Karteros, and the beaches of Aghia Pelaghia, Linoperamata, Ammoudara, Gouves, Analipsis, Limenas Chersonissou, Stalida etc.

On the southern coast: Kokkinos Pyrgos, Kalamaki, Kommos, Matala, Kaloi Limenes, Lentas, Tsoutsouros, Keratokampos, Avri and others.

The sea around Letnas and Tsoutsouros is good for *harpooning*. There are *water-skiing* and *wind-surfing* schools at Limenas Chersonissou, at Mallia and Aghia Pelaghia.

At the beaches most frequented by tourists there are pedal boats, canoes, equipment for water-sports etc. for hire.

The larger hotels have swimming pools, *tennis* courts, *mini-golf* courts, and every kind of equipment for water sports.

At Herakleion there is a covered swimming pool as well as *basket-ball* and *volley-ball* courts, *tennis* courts and a covered gymnasium.

On *Psiloritis* there are two slopes, one large and one small.

A *marina* where yachts can refuel and take on water is available in the port of Herakleion.

Kaloi Limenes also has refuelling facilities and at Limenas Chersonissou there is a harbour where yachts can moor.

Herakleion port serves boats entering or leaving Greece. Port, customs and health authorities are stationed here, as well as a passport and foreign exchange control office. Also available at Herakleion is a work–shop for the repair and maintenance of yachts.

Local products - Shopping

From the mountain villages of the province one can buy the delicious gruyère-type Cretan cheese, sweet-smelling "myzithra" and "anthotyro" (both white cheeses). There are folk art shops in all the villages frequented by tourists. At Zaro one can find beautiful handwoven articles.

At Hekaleion, on 1821 Street and on Kalokaiinou Avenue, there are still the old "knife–shops" where one can buy the traditional Cretan daggers.

Also in town there are shops selling leather goods as well as many jewellery shops selling beautiful items, some of which are faithful copies of the magnificent Minoan and Byzantine jewellery which one can admire in the museums. There are also jewellery shops in many of the popular

tourist villages, especially those of the northern coast of the province. Copper/bronze, terracota, wooden and other souvenirs are sold almost everywhere.

Local festivals and cultural events
Herakleion: July 1 – September 15: "Herakleion Summer Festival".
The Municipality of Herakleion has been organizing this event for several years. It includes concerts, song recitals, choral singing, dance performances (Greek, foreign, modern, folk groups), theatre, fine arts exhibitions, and other events.
The festival takes place in the following venues:
– the Kazantzakis Garden – Theatre
– the Little Municipal Garden – Theatre (next to the above)
– the Municipal Theatre – in the port
– the Koule Fortress
– the Basilica of Saint Mark
– the Domenikos Theotokopoulos Hall, near the Morosini fountain.
During the winter season there is also a variety of events including plays, concerts, lectures etc, organized by the Municipality and local cultural associations.
In the town of Herakleion, the following traditional festivities take place:
August 25, feast of Saint Titus
November 11, feast of Saint Minas

In several other villages of the Prefecture, the local cultural associations organize various events between the end of July and the middle of August.

USEFUL TELEPHONE NUMBERS (081)

Directory enquiries Crete	131
Herakleion Fire Brigade	199
Emergency Services of Herakleion	100
Herakleion Municipality	399399
National Tourist Organization of Greece	228203
Municipal Police	221540
Tourist Police	283190
Port Authority	108 • 244912
Airport	228402
Herakleion Olympic Airways	229191
Herakleion Hotels Association	288108
Herakleion Tourist Coaches Association	223535
KTEL Regional Buses	245019
Hospital (Venizeleion)	237502
University Hospital	392111
Apolloneion Medical Centre	229713
Emergency Aid Service	166 • 222222

LASITHI PREFECTURE

How to get there

By car–ferry from Piraeus: There are three ferry–boat services a week in the summer and two in the winter from Piraeus to the island of Milos, to Aghios Nikolaos and Siteia.

The trip takes 12 hours to Aghios Nikolaos and approximately one more hour to Siteia. Twice a week the ferries continue their journey to the islands of Kasos, Karpathos and Rhodes in the Dodecanese.

By air from Athens: The Prefecture is served by the airports of Herakleion and Siteia. Siteia is linked twice a week to Athens (flight time: 1 hr. 15 mins.) and once a week to Karpathos (flight time 30 mins). The airport is only 1 km. away from the town and passengers can use urban buses, Olympic Airways coaches or taxis.

By road. The Lasithi KTEL buses link the three large towns (Aghios Nikolaos, Siteia, Ierapetra) with the majority of the villages of the Prefecture. Also, starting from these three large towns, Lasithi is linked to Herakleion, Rethymnon and Chania.

Local connections by sea. The islet of *Spinalonga* is reached by special caïques starting from Aghios Nikolaos, Elounda and Plaka.

The islet of *Chrysi,* on the Libyan Sea opposite Ierapetra (distance: 11 nautical miles) is connected by caïque to the port of Ierapetra).

Car and motorcycle rentals. Taxis.
At Aghios Nikolaos, Elounda, Siteia, Ierapetra and at all the places popular with tourists there are shops renting cars and motorcycles.

Tourist Agencies. There are many agencies, not only in the three main towns, but also in the various villages frequented by tourists.

**Entertainment – Sports –
Leisure Activities.**
In every corner of the prefecture there are all sorts of places where one can eat or enjoy an evening out. They cater every taste, even to that of the most demanding customer, and range from elegant cosmopolitan restaurants to popular little tavernas and coffee shops, from busy discos to small intimate bars with a lot of atmosphere.

Most of the beaches are clean and suitable for *swimming*. At Aghios Nikolaos there are two municipal beaches which are very popular. Near the town are the beaches of Ammoudi, Havania and Ammoudara. On the northern coast: Sisi, Milatos, Vlihadia, Plaka, Elounda, Schisma. In Mirabello Bay: Istros, Pacheia Ammos. There are beaches at Mochlos, on the little island of Aghios Nikolaos across the bay, at Faneromeni, in the Bay of Siteia (Petras, Aghia Fotia) and, finally, there is the unique beach of the Palm Tree Grove (Finikodasos), with its golden sands, on the northeastern point of Crete.

On the eastern side of the island are the beaches of Angathia, Chiona, Kouremero - near Palaekastro, while on the southern coast are the endless beaches from Makrygialos to Myrtos, which are washed by the Libyan Sea. Lovely crystal–clear seas and superb beaches are also to be found on the little island of Chrysi opposite Ierapetra.

Around the small islands of Spinalonga and Chrysi the seas are particulary suitable for *fishing*, also near Mochlos and Palaekastro. At Aghios Nikolaos, Elounda, Siteia, Ierapetra and other places there are shops renting accessories for water sports. There are also skiffs, and pedal–boats for hire at many of the beaches.

The large hotel complexes of the area have *tennis courts*.

At Aghios Nikolaos there is a *National Swimming Pool* where swimming contests are held.

The National Stadium (sports grounds) of Aghios Nikolaos is equipped with basket–ball and volley–ball courts.

Private yachts can moor in the harbours of Aghios Nikolaos, Siteia and Ierapetra. At Aghios Nikolaos there are boat repair workshops.

Local Products – Shopping.

There are many shops in the town and tourist centres of Lasithi which sell souvenirs and traditional handmade articles.

At Kritsa one can find delicate embroidery, handwoven articles and small woodcarved decorative objects.

The jewellery shops in Aghios Nikolaos have a beautiful selection of items.

Local events – festivals.

Aghios Nikolaos: The coming of the New Year is celebrated with festivities and distribution of gifts. At Easter, a platform is set up in the middle of the lake, where the "burning of Judas" takes place. This is quite a spectacular Easter custom.

In the summer, the Municipal Cultural Centre of Aghios Nikolaos organizes a cultural event called "Lato" whith a varied programme which includes plays for adults and children, music, dancing etc. Local groups take part, as well as groups from all over Greece.

Elounda: in the summer, cultural events are organized by the local Cultural Association.

Ieraptera: July–August, cultural events, called the "Corvia". They include dance performances, concerts, exhibitions etc.

Kritsa: August 15, service celebrated in the Byzantine church of Panghia Kera.

Toplou monastery: Ressurection service celebrated with great solemnity in the monastery.

Neapolis: August 15, Assumption day, village festival.

Lasithi Plateau: many genuine traditional festivals take place in the area of the Lasithi plateau.

Siteia: In the summer months the Municipality organizes cultural vents under the title "Kornareia".
August 15–20 "Sultana Raisin Festival".

USEFUL TELEPHONE NUMBERS

AGHIOS NIKOLAOS (0841)

Municipality of Ag. Nikolaos	25330
National Tourist Organization of Greece	22357
Tourist Police	22251 • 26900
Port Authority	22312
Hospital	25221
KTEL	22234

IERAPETRA (0842)

Police	22560
Port Authority	22294
Hospital	22488

SITEIA (0843)

Police	22266
Port Authority	22310
Hospital	24311–2

PREFECTURE OF RETHYMNON

How to get there:

By car-ferry from Piraeus:
Rethymnon is linked by boat to Piraeus. The trip takes approximately 11 hours.

By air from Athens and Thessaloniki.
There are no direct flights from Rethymnon to Ahtens and Thessaloniki. The town is serviced by the airport of Chania. The distance between Rethymnon and Chania is 68 kms. and passengers can take the Olympic Airways coach (services are timed to correspond with one or two flights a day) of the KTEL interurban buses.

By road. The road network in the Rethymnon Prefecture is good and there are regular urban and interurban bus services linking Rethymnon to the rest of the island.

Local communications by sea. There are regular services by small caïques, in the summer, starting from Plakias to Aghios Pavlos, Aghia Galini, Peveli. Twice a week in the summer there are also excursions to Santorini by cruise ship. The trip takes approximately 5 hours.

Car and motorcycle rental. Taxis.
There are agencies in town, in several villages and local communities of the Prefecture. A large fleet of taxis is also available.

Tourist Agencies. There are several tourist agencies in town and in the majority of the most popular seaside resorts, which organize excursions to the sights of the islands.

Entertainment - Sports - Leisur activities.
There are many places in Rethymnon itself and even in the more remote villages, where one can have a simple meal or enjoy delicious local specialities or foreign cuisine.
Entertainment in the evenings is guaranteed: there are bars, music bars, discos, cabarets, places where one can listen to popular or bouzouki music, or where Cretan songs and dances are performed.
The prefecture of Rethymnon has many lovely beaches for *swimming*.
Along the northern coast: Petres – to the west of Rethymnon town – Perivolia, Platanes, Stavromenos, Panormos, Bali – to the east of the town.

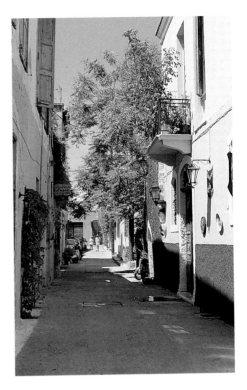

On the southern coast: Aghia Galini, Aghios Pavlos, Aghios Georgios, Preveli, Plakias, Korakas, Polyrizo, etc.

For fishing enthusiasts, the coastal region around Plakias, Aghia Galini, Panormo, is recommended.

Water sports can be enjoyed at the large hotels.

At the more popular beaches there are also shops renting the necessary accessories for water-skiing and wind-surfing; canoes and pedal-boats can also be hired.

Rethymnon has a *national stadium*, as well as basket-ball and volley-ball courts and football grounds.

There are football pitches in many of the villages. Some of the large hotel complexes also include *tennis courts* and *mini-golfs courses*.

For those who enjoy *mountaineering,* the Rethymnon Mountaineering Association offers the use of an organized refuge at the site called Toumbotos Prinos, at an altitude of 1, 650 m.

Facilities for the berthing of *private yachts* are available in the harbour of Rethymnon, at Aghia Galini and Panormos.

Local products –Shopping.

Rethymnon is famous for its beautiful traditional embroidery and good quality handwoven articles, which the shopper will be able to find in shops in town and, in the case of handwoven articles, at Anogheia and Zoniana.

One cal also buy excellent gruyère–type cheese, myzithra and anthotyro (local white cheese) from the mountain villages in the Prefecture and from shops in Rethymnon itself.

In the folk-art shops one can choose woodcarvings, leather goods, copper bronze articles or pottery -mostly decorative objects- while one can find very beautiful and elegant items in the jewellery shops.

At the village of Margarites there is a potter's workshop, and one can also buy the delicious local honey.

Local events and traditional festivals.

Rethymnon: Carnival time is celebrated in Rethymnon with masquerades, danced, songs, and plenty of fun.

End of July, Wine Festival in the Municipal Gardens. End of July – first ten days in August, Rethymnon Renaissance Festival. The cultural events include concerts, theatre and dance performances, pantomimes and pageants in Renaissance style. During this period the town is decked out in flags and is pervaded by a genuine Renaissance atmosphere. Most of the events take place in the Fortezza theatre.

November 8, National Day to commemorate the Arkadi Holocaust.

Anogheia: Ascension day herdsmen's festival. Mid–August: "Anogheia" - cultural activities.

August 15, celebration of the Assumption of the Holy Virgin.

Panormos: Carnival – "Clean Monday" (first day of Lent), local traditional Carnival. Summer: cultural events with Cretan evenings.

Arkadi Monastery: November 8, commemoration of the Arkadi Holocaust.

USEFUL TELEPHONE NUMBERS (0831)

Information of the Phone Book of Crete	131
Rethymnon Fire Brigade	199
Emergency Aid Service	166
Rethymnon Municipality	22245
National Tourist Organization of Greece	29148 · 56350
Police	22289
Tourist Police	53450 · 28156
Port Authority	22276
KTEL Regional Buses	22212
Olympic Airways	22257
Hospital	27491
Arkadi Monastery	83076

PREFECTURE OF CHANIA

How to get there

By car-ferry from Piraeus to Souda:
These are daily services – more frequent in the summer and less so in the winter – from Piraeus to Souda. The distance is 157 naut. miles and the voyage takes approximately eleven hours. The port of Souda is at a distance of 7 kms. from Chania to which it is linked by local buses.

By car-ferry from Piraeus to Kastelli Kissamou:
There are two services a week, via Monemvasia, Neapolis, Gytheion – on the mainland of the Peloponnese – the island of Kythera (Aghia Pelaghia – Kapsali), and the island of Antikythera.

By air from Athens.
There are frequent daily flights from Athens to Chania in the summer, less frequent ones in the winter. The flight lasts approximately 45 mins. and the airport is 15.2 kms from the town. For their transportation, passengers can use the urban bus services, the airport buses of Olympic Airways, or taxis.

By air from Thessaloniki.
There is one flight a week from Thessaloniki. The flight takes one and a quarter hours. There are daily charter flights which link Chania to many European cities during the tourist season.

By road
Chania is well served by urban and interurban buses.
Local boat services: from: Chora Sfakion to Loutro – Aghia Roumeli – Soughia – Palaeochora.
From *Chora Sfakion* to the island of Gavdos.
From *Palaeochora* to the island of Gavdos. There are two services a week by ferry – boat from *Gytheion* in the Peloponnese to Kastelli Kissamou. The trip takes approximately 6 hours.

Hiring of cars, motorcycles – taxis.
There are many car and motorcycle rental agencies in Chania, in Souda, at the airport and in several villages. The putlie's needs are also well served by a large fleet of taxis.

Tourist agencies.
There are plentiful in Chania and in the various villages frequented by tourists. They also organize excursions to the various interesting sites of the island.

Entertainment – Sports – Leisure activities.
There is no shortage of restaurants, tavernas, pizza parlours, ouzo bars, restaurants serving foreign cuisine or tavernas with local specialities, fresh seafood, and fast food: there is also a vegetarian restaurant.
One can enjoy oneself until the early hours of the morning in the numerous pubs, discos, bars, night–clubs with bouzouki music or traditional Cretan music, and cabarets, in and around Chania. The town has several winter and summer (outdoor) cinemas.
The Regional Theatre of Crete performs plays as does the Chania Theatrical Workshop and travelling theatre companies.
In the majority of the villages in the Prefecture, especially those most frequ-

ented by tourists, one can also find many places offering food and entertainment.

Good beaches for *swimming* in the vicinity of the town are: the whole of the western coast up to Kolymbari and, to the east, the beaches of Aptera, Kalami, Kalyves, Almyrida, Plaka. Also, at Akrotiri: Kalathas, Stavros, Marathi, Aghios Nikolaos.

All the beaches in the Prefecture are suitable for swimming.

The best beaches on the Libyan Sea are those of Aghia Roumeli, Frangocastello, Chora Sfakion, Loutro, Soughia, Palaeochora, Trachili. Near Palaeochora are situated the wonderful beaches of Pacheia Ammos, Chalikia, Kountroura, and the three nudist beaches of Anhydroi, Psilos Volakas and Krios.

On the western coast of the Prefecture: Falasarna, Sfinari, Ormos Stomiou, Elafonissi.

Near Kastelli Kissamou, the beaches of Nopigheia and Drapanias.

Sailing, swimming, water–skiing and diving schools are operated by the Chania Yacht Club. The Chania National Centre for Water Sports is on Akti Kanari.

On the beaches most popular with holiday–makers one can find shops selling all the necessary accessories for wind–surfing, canoeing, pedal–boating and other water sports.

For *fishing* the best places are the rocky beaches at Sfakia and Soughia, and to the west the area of Falasarna and Sfinari.

There are *tennis courts* at Chania, near the airport, and in the large hotels.

The *Chania National Stadium* has basket - and volley - ball courts and a gymnasium.

Mountaineering – Skiing: There are small ski runs on the White Mountains. At Kallergi peak there is a mountain refuge.

Private yachts can be berthed at the ports of Chania, Souda, Kastelli and Palaeohora. Boat repairs can be carried out in Chania. The authorities of the port of Chania can check boats entering and leaving Greece.

Local products – Shopping

Local cheeses from the shops in Chania and from mountain villages. Also raki and sweet-scented honey.

In the folk-art shops in Chania and in villages frequented by tourists, a variety of souvenirs are for sale.

There are also many jewellery shops in Chania and several shops selling leather goods. Here one can also buy the traditional high Cretan boots ("stivania"), in the "stivanadika" shops.

Local festivals and events

Chania: in May, athletic contests are organized, called the "Venizelia". In August the Chania Prefecture organizes cultural events including a varied programme and exhibitions.
Vammos: Beginning of August: cultural events with concerts, dance programmes, singing, and exhibitions.
Kastelli: August, cultural events, the "Gramvousia", which include musical evenings, exhibitions etc.
Maleme: May, commemoration of the Battle of Crete.
Palaeochora: beginning of August, cultural events, "Musical August".
Frangocastello: September 15, feast-day of Aghios Nikitas.

Chrysoskalitissa: August 15, Assumption of the Holy Virgin traditional fest at the monastery.

USEFUL TELEPHONE NUMBERS (0821)

Directory enquiries Crete	131
Emergency Aid Service	166
Chania Municipality	92000
National Tourist Organization of Greece	92943
Chania Police	28744
Tourist Police	73333
Souda Police	89316
Airport	63224
Olympic Airways of Chania	53760
KTEL Urban Buses	27044
KTEL Regional Buses	91288
Chania Port Authority	98888
Souda Port Authority	89240
Chania Red Cross	52550
Chania Hospital	27000
Naval Hospital of Crete (Souda)	89307

ACCOMMODATION

Accommodation of various types and categories is available throughout the island. There are hotels designated as Luxury class, A, B, C, D, and E class, bungalows, furnished flats, pensions, rooms to rent, even luxury villas. There are camp sites at several places, especially seaside resorts.

Information:
Local Information Offices of the municipalities and of the National Tourist Organisation of Greece. Local Police Stations.

Information–bookings:
Greek Hotels Association.
a) Main Offices:
   Stadiou 24, Athens,
   Tel. 2103310022
   Fax. 2103236962

b) Branch Office:
   Stadiou and Karayiorghi Servias 2,
   Syntagma Square,
   (National Bank of Greece)
   Tel. 2103237193

* Several hotels – mainly those which are situated outside the towns, along the coast – operate from April to October.

NOTE:
The information on hotels has been taken from published by the Hotels Association of Greece, "GREEK HOTELS 1999". Information on camp sites has been provided by the National Tourist Organization of Greece.

CATEG.	NAME	TEL.	BEDS
	IRAKLIO		
	AGIA PELAGIA (2810)		
L	CAPSIS BEACH	811112	1228
A	ALEXANDE HOUSE	811303	147
A (f.a.)	AQUARIUS	811614	34
A (f.a.)	IRINI	–	20
A (h.-b.)	PENINSULA	811313	367
A (f.a.)	SKALA	811333	40
B	MONONAFTIS	289404	74
B	PANORAMA	811002	254
B (f.a.)	PERLA	811034	63
B	STELIOS	811071/2	76
C (f.a.)	ANATOLI	811017	20
C (f.a.)	EVA MARE I	811186	18
C (f.a.)	EVA MARE II	811186	19
C	HARIS	–	81
C (f.a.)	THALIA	–	36
D (f.a.)	EVI	811167	19
D (f.a.)	LADY M	811533	6
D (f.a.)	MIROS	–	30
D (f.a.)	NITSA	811067	9
	AMNISSOS (2810)		
B	KARTEROS	3804402	105
C	PRINCE OF LILLIES	225822	57
	AMOUDARA (2810)		
L	CANDIA MARIS	314632	596
A	AGAPI BEACH VIP	311084	24
A	CRETA BEACH	252302	265
A	DOPHIN BAY	821276/7	500
A	GRECOTEL AGAPI BEACH	311084	391
A	SANTA MARINA BEACH	261103	398
B	AGAPI VILLAGE	311084	199
B	CORALI BEACH	260909	72
B	LAMBI	821915/7	209
B	MARILENA	254312	251
C (f.a.)	ANGELA	250660	22
C	GORGONA	821920	73
C (f.a.)	LYKTOS	285211	36
C	MINOAS	821557	67
C	OSTRIA	831371	20
C	SANTA ELENA	251770	127
C	TSANGARAKIS BEACH	251768	83
C	VIOLETA	250773	33
D (f.a.)	KOSTAS MARIA	250898	28
D (f.a.)	PALMYRA	821534	42
E	GORTIS	251778	219
	ANO VIANNOS (28950)		
A	VIANNOS	–	45
	ARKALOHORI (28910)		
D	EFTHIMIA	23554	16
	ARVI (28950)		
C	ARIADNI	71300	22
	DAFNES (2810)		
B (tr.h.)	KONSTANTINA		6
	GOURNES (2810)		
A	EVINA	761034	62
A (f.a.)	GOLDEN BAY	761866/8	62
A (f.a.)	KRITZAS	762001/3	98
A (f.a.)	RENATA	761170	56
B	ROYAL	761234/5	126
C	ERATO	761277	60
C (f.a.)	KRI-KRI VILLAGE	761063	60
	GOUVES (28970)		
A	APHRODITE BEACH	41102	482
A	ASTIR BEACH	41141/2	211
A	DIOGENIS PALACE	42770	129

CATEG.	NAME	TEL.
A	EL GRECO	–
A	GRECOTEL CRETA SUN	41103
A (f.a.)	KLIO	41189
A	MAGDA	42307/8
A	MARINA	41112
A (f.a.)	MAYA BEACH	42592/4
A	PANTHEON PALACE	42025
A	STUDIOS LIDA	41456
A (f.a.)	SWEET MEMORY	–
B	APOLLO	41102
B	BYRON	41130
B (f.a.)	CHRISTI APARTMENTS	–
B	GOUVES BAY	42756
B	HARA ILIOS VILLAGE	42740/1
C	CALYPSO HOLIDAYS	41390
C	DESPO	41242
	EDERI	41204
C	GOUVES SEA	41401
C	IRENE	–
C (f.a.)	KAISSA BEACH	41800/2
C	KOUROS	42350
C	LAVRIS	41101
C	SONIA	41430
	HANI KOKINI (2810)	
A (f.a.)	ANNA	761691
A (h.-b.)	ARINA SAND	761135
A (f.a.)	CORALI BEACH	761858
A (h.-b.)	KNOSSOS BEACH	761000
A (f.a.)	MARY VILLAGE	–
A	RINELA BEACH	761713
A	THEMIS BEACH	761412
B (f.a.)	SUNSET	761553
B	XENIA-ILIOS	761502
C	AKTI	761260
C	COSMAN	–
C	DANAE	761375
C	DIONYSSOS	761371
C	KAMARI	761002
C (f.a.)	PELA MARE	762000
C	PRIMA	761512
	IRAKLIO (2810)	
A	ASTORIA	229002
A	ATLANTIS	229103
A	FODELE BEACH	521251/5
A	GALAXY	238812
A	MINOA PALACE	380404/6
A	XENIA	284000/4
B	ATRION	229225
B	ESPERIA	228534
B	KASTRO	284185
B	LATO	228103
B	MEDITERRANEAN	289331/4
B	PETRA	229912
C	APOLLON	250025
C	ARES	280646
C	ATHINAIKON	229312
C	CASTELLO	251212
C	DAEDALOS	244812/5
C	EL GRECO	281071/5
C	EVANS	223928
C	GRABELES	241205/8
C	HERACLEION	281881/3
C	ILAIRA	227103
C	IRENE	229703
C	KRETA	282238
C	KRIS	223211
C	KRONOS	282240

NAME	TEL.	BEDS
MARINI	220737	87
MIRABELLO	285052	42
OASSIS	254082	35
OLYMPIC	288861/4	135
ARKADI	282077	29
IKAROS (ex Monderno)	283006	83
LIFE	243090	34
PHAESTOS	283027	41
REA	223638	37
SAN GIORGIO	92265	39
ARGO	254588	54
ARIADNE	255765	43
ATLAS	288989	30
LENA	223280	31
PALLADION	282563	45
STAR	252367	19
KAMILARI (28920)		
OASSIS	42217	23
KARTEROS (2810)		
AMNISSOS	281332/5	147
.) SEMELI	–	23
KARTEROS ELEAS (2810)		
.) MINOS BAY	289379	68
KASTELI PEDIADOS (28910)		
KALLIOPI	32685	20
KATO GOUVES (28970)		
ST. CONSTANTIN I	42752/4	67
ST. CONSTANTIN II	42752/4	73
.) MARIYANNA	41370/1	74
KOKINOS PIRGOS (28920)		
FILIPPOS	52555	86
LIBYAN SEA	51621	42
LITTLE INN	51400	87
MARY-ELEN	51268	113
TA ADELFIA	51462	20
EL GRECO	51182	19
KOUTLOULOUFARI (28970)		
.) VILLA IPPOKAMPI	22316	30
LENTAS (28920)		
) LENTAS	95221, 25221/223	
LIMENAS HERSONISSOU (28970)		
ANNABEL VILLAGE	23561/4	530
BELLA MARIS	21410/5	324
b.) CRETA MARIS	22115/30	1078
HERSONISSOS PALACE	23603	270
KNOSSOS ROYAL VILLAGE	23575	840
PARADISE	22893	82
ROYAL MARE VILLAGE	25025	854
.) ACROPOLIS	22172	58
ANISSA BEACH	23264/7	550
.) ARLEN BEACH	–	22
.) ARTEMIS	23570	36
.) ATHINA INN	23765	36
CRETAN VILLAGE	22997	610
.) CRISTI	–	34
.) EASET APARTMENTS	22850/6	74
EUROPA BEACH	21530/4	406
EVELYN BEACH	24635/6	142
.) FOUR SEASONS	–	34
.) GALAXY VILLAS	22910	119
GOLDENBEACH	22368	217
.) KASTRI VILLAGE	22102	40
-b.) KING MINOS PALACE	22881	253
.) KOUTOULOUFARI APART.	22688	87
LYTTOS	22575/8	601

CATEG.	NAME	TEL.	BEDS
A	NANA BEACH	22950	502
A (f.a.)	NENA	22196	22
A (f.a.)	ORION	–	33
A (f.a.)	PALATIA VILLAGE	22017	80
A (h.-b.)	PEFANA VILLAGE	22548/9	129
A	ROYAL BELVEDERE	22371	665
A (f.a.)	SANDIKA	–	12
A	SEMIRAMIS VILLAGE	21005	302
A	SERITA BEACH	24542	479
A	SILVA MARIS	22850/6	433
A	SUNSHINE VILLAGE HERSONISSOS	25136/8	145
A (f.a.)	WEST APARTMENTS	22850/6	26
A (B.)	ZORBAS VILLAGE	23268/71	386
B	AGRABELLA	23110/1	194
B	ALBATROS	22144	214
B (f.a.)	ALEKA-NANCIA	22485	28
B (f.a.)	ALIA	23146	84
B (f.a.)	ARIANE	22536	137
B (f.a.)	ASSITES	22968	20
B	BIZANTIUM	24430	60
B	CHRYSSI AMMOUDIA	22971/2	342
B	CRETAN PHILOXENIA - NIKOS BEACH	–	113
B (f.a.)	DEDALOS VILLAGE	22666	106
B (f.a.)	DIANA	–	36
B	DIMITRION	22220	173
B (f.a.)	ELPIDA HERSONISSOU	22869	28
B	ERI BEACH	22271/5	446
B	GLAROS	22106	304
B (f.a.)	HARIS	22346	36
B	HERONISSOS	22501	221
B	HERSONISSOS MARIS	22400	216
B (f.a.)	IDILIO	–	8
B (f.a.)	IOKASTI	22607	48
B	MARAGAKIS	22405	102
B (f.a.)	MARIA	22580	68
B	OCEANIS	22671/2	248
B (f.a.)	PHAEDRA HERSONISSOU	–	26
B (f.a.)	PORTO GRECO	–	52
B	SERGIOS	22583/5	181
B	SOFIA	25150/1	53
B	STELLA VILLAGE	–	218
B	THALIA	22590/1	93
B	VENUS MELENA	22892	92
B (f.a.)	VILLES ESPERIDES	22322	98
C	ADAMAKIS	22447	39
C	ADONIS	22141	22
C (f.a.)	ALEKOS	22110	14
C	ALOE	22938	45
C (f.a.)	ALONI	22562	9
C	ANGELOS	22258	23
C	ANGELOS VILLAGE	–	122
C	ANNA	22753	82
C (f.a.)	ANNIRIN	–	26
C (f.a.)	ANNITA	–	22
C	ANTINOOS	24446	60
C	ARMAVA	22544	76
C (f.a.)	ASPRA	22889	12
C	ASPETIS	22062	24
C	AVERINOS	22994	76
C	AVRA	22203	32
C (f.a.)	BELLA VISTA	24577	52
C	BLUE ISLAND	21545	68
C	BLUE SKY	22208	41
C	DANELIS	22155	124
C (f.a.)	DASSIA	–	28

CATEG.	NAME	TEL.	BEDS
C	DESPINA	22966	32
C	DIKTYNA	22648	72
C	DIMICO	22697	85
C	DIMITRA	22685	78
C (f.a.)	ELENI	24690	23
C	EVA	22090/2	62
C (f.a.)	FILIPPAKIS	22165	37
C	FLISVOS	22006	118
C	FLORAL	23004	43
C	GALINI	22207	98
C (f.a.)	HAPINESS APTS	–	28
C	HELEANA	22830	34
C	HELENA	22226	24
C (f.a.)	HERCULES	22527	21
C	ILIOS	22500	151
C	IRO	22136	98
C	KAMELIA	24559	18
C (f.a.)	KASSAVETIS G	23052/4	114
C (f.a.)	KATERINA	22304	34
C	KOSTA MARE	22297	111
C (f.a.)	KRITIKOS ASTERAS	–	89
C	LENA-MARY	22907	28
C	MAISTRALI	22133	35
C	MARIANA	22709	94
C	MARIE-CHRISTINE	22537	115
C	MARIE-GEORGE	22991	41
C (f.a.)	MARIETA	–	32
C	MARIETA II	22081	50
C (f.a.)	MARITA	22310	29
C	MASTORAKIS	22965	26
C	MELPO	22350	77
C	MEMORY	22497	61
C (f.a.)	MINAS	–	41
C	MIRAMARE	22796	93
C	NANCY	22212	49
C	NIKI	22379	58
C	OASSIS	21787/8	76
C	PALMERA BEACH	22481/3	134
C	PARASKEVI	–	31
C	PELA-MARIA	22195	224
C	PERAKIS	22968	21
C (f.a.)	PERIGHIALI	–	52
C (f.a.)	PETRA BEACH	23060	45
C (f.a.)	PISKOPIANO	22726	84
C (f.a.)	PLAZA	22760	39
C	PSARROS	22534	47
C	REA	22357	29
C (f.a.)	ROMANTICA	24809	38
C (f.a.)	SOFI	22557	18
C (f.a.)	SOGIORKA	–	53
C	SOLANO	–	34
C (f.a.)	SONIA MARE	–	48
C (f.a.)	SOUTH KASSAVETIS	23410/1	119
C (f.a.)	STELIOS	22046	35
C (f.a.)	STELLA	22016	25
C	SUN MARINE	24623	24
C	THEODORA	23158	39
C (f.a.)	TSALOS BEACH	24414	36
C	VASSO	22047	74
C	VELISSARIOS	22259	43
C	VENUS	23369	93
C (f.a.)	VILLA MARGARITA	22610	43
C	VIRGINIA	22466	18
C	VOULA	22097	32
C	VRITO	22401	32
C (f.a.)	YANNADAKIS	22937	16
C	ZORBAS	22075	46

CATEG.	NAME	TEL.	BEDS
D	ARGO	22978	22
D (f.a.)	DORIAN	22421	22
D (f.a.)	MANOS	22016	32
D	MILIOTAKIS	23081	16
D (f.a.)	NEFELI	41315	14
D (f.a.)	VILLA MEDOUSSA	22624	32
LINOPERAMATA (2810)			
A	APOLLONIA BEACH	821624	590
A	ZEUS BEACH	821503	717
LYGARIA AHLADAS (2810)			
L	ATHINA PALACE	811800	680
C (f.a.)	FTERIA	811620	101
MALIA (28970)			
A	GRECOTEL	32301/3	378
	MALIA PARK	–	
A	IKAROS VILLAGE	31267/9	354
A	KERNOS BEACH	31421/5	519
A	KYKNOS	32040	160
A	SARPIDON	32873	85
A	SIRENS BEACH	31321/4	466
A	SIRENS VILLAGE	31321	134
B	ALEXANDER BEACH	32134	518
B	ANASTASIA	31180	74
B	ARIADNE	31592	97
B	ARIADNI BEACH	31592	96
B (b.)	CALYPSO	31012	86
B	COSTAS	31485/7	64
B (tr.f.a.)	KOSMIMA MALLION	–	9
B	MALIA BAY	–	273
B	MALIA BEACH	31003	504
B	MALIA DEDALOS	32780/1	76
B	MALLIOTAKIS BEACH	–	51
B	MATHEO	–	86
B	NICOELEN	–	66
B (f.a.)	NIRIIDES	32028	38
B	PHAEDRA BEACH	31560/1	255
B	TRITON	32210	44
C	ALTIS	31757	33
C	AMVROSSIA	31378	54
C	ARTEMIS	31583	68
C	CHRISTIANA BEACH	31369	156
C	CLEO	31112	32
C	DIONYSSOS	31475	76
C	EFI	31640	37
C	ELKOMI	31595	82
C	FRIXOS	31941	70
C (tr.f.a.)	GHIANNIS-MARIA	31313	20
C	HELEN	31545	43
C	HERMES	31788	121
C	ILMA	–	49
C (f.a.)	KONI	–	72
C	MALIA HOLIDAYS	31206	206
C	MALIA MARE	31809	64
C (f.a.)	MALIA STUDIOS	31655	27
C	MARIA-ROUSSE	32708	63
C	MINOA	31456	37
C	MINOA SUN	31456	21
C	MISTRAL	31934/5	70
C	MOONLIGHT	–	34
C	NEON	33206/8	133
C	PASSIPHAE	–	37
C	SOFOCLES BEACH	31348	84
C (f.a.)	SUN BEACH	31557	57
C	SUNSHINE	31401	49
C	THEODORA	–	14
C	VERGAS	31606	67
C (f.a.)	VILLA ROZA	–	18

CATEG.	NAME	TEL.	BEDS
C	WINDMILL	31645	41
D	ALKYON	31394	26
D	ARCADI	31439	44
D	ARGO	31636	50
D	ARMONIA	31490	39
D	BANANIES	31203	26
D	DROSSIA	31275	36
D	DROSSIA II	31656	61
D (f.a.)	EVITA	32635	17
D	GRAMMATIKAKI	31366	91
D	HERA	31554	26
D	MARYELEN	31419	34
D	SWEET DREAMS	–	41
D (f.a.)	VILLA MALIA	31002	34
D	ZEUS	31464	70
E	ARCHONTI	31555	16
E	ERMIONI	31093	17
E	GERANI	31518	20
E	IBISCUS	31313	18
E	IRINI	31658/9	21
E	OASSIS	31470	60
E	POPI	31457	16
E	THEONI	31341	36
MATALA (28920)			
B	ARMONIA	45735	47
B	VALLEY VILLAGE	45776	86
C	CALYPSO	42792	35
C	EVA-MARINA	45125	40
C	FRANGISKOS	45380	69
C	MARINA	42793	39
C	MATALA BAY	45100	104
C	ORION	42129	103
C	PRINGIPISSA EVROPI	45113	72
C	SUN	42146	54
C	ZAFIRIA II	45112	113
D	CHEZ XENOPHON	42358	43
D	ZAFIRIA	45112	19
E	NIKOS (ex Coral)	42375	41
E	ROMANTICA	45357	20
E	SCORPIOS	42102	26
E	SOFIA	45134	24
MIRES (28920)			
D	OLYMPIC	22777	30
NEA ALIKARNASSOS (2810)			
B	ASTERION	227913	84
C	SOFIA	240002	94
PALEOKASTRO (2810)			
C	ROGDIA	821373	42
D (f.a.)	EGAGROS	841334	39
PISKOPIANO (28970)			
B (f.a.)	KALIMERA	–	44
B (f.a.)	PANORAMA	22502	74
B (f.a.)	STELVA I	22890	24
B (f.a.)	VILLES MIKA	22983	28
C (f.a.)	EDELWEIS	22631	24
C (f.a.)	KORIFI I	23063	30
C (f.a.)	KORIFI II	23331	22
E	ANDRIANI	22756	36
POROS (2810)			
C	GLORIA	245412	95
C	PASSIPHAE	245392	32
C	POSEIDON	245360	49
SERVILI TILISSOU (2810)			
A (b.)	AROLITHOS	821050	62
STALIDA (28970)			
A	ANTHOUSSA BEACH	31380/2	321
A (f.a.)	CRETA SOLARIS	31496	30

CATEG.	NAME	TEL.
A (f.a.)	ILISSIA PEDIA	32090
A (f.a.)	LATANIA	31556
A (f.a.)	PENELOPE	31370
A (f.a.)	PRIMAVERA	31591
A (f.a.)	RESIDENCE	31528
B	ALKYONIDES	31558
B (f.a.)	AMAZONES VILLAS	31488
B (b.)	BLUE SEA	31371
B	CACTUS BEACH	32494/7
B	DIAMOND BEACH	–
B	HORIZON BEACH	24661/3
B	KATRIN	32137/40
B	KORINA	31057
B	MARLENA	31555
B	PALM BEACH	31666
B	SUNNY BEACH	31587
B	ZEPHYROS BEACH	31691/3
C (f.a.)	CAPTAIN'S VILLA	31593
C	ELVIRA	31634
C	HELIOTROPE	31515/7
C (f.a.)	L'AMOUR	31615
C (f.a.)	NIKI	31964
C	PANORAMA STALIDOS	31958/9
C (f.a.)	SAMMI	–
C	SMARAGDINE BEACH	31952
C	THISVI	31969
C (f.a.)	VILLA ANNA	31506
C (f.a.)	VILLA MARIA	31450
C (f.a.)	VILLA RITSA	31492
C	ZERVAS BEACH	32719
D (f.a.)	ARMINDA	22486
D (f.a.)	MARIANDY	–
D	STALIS	31246
D (f.a.)	VILLA MATAMY	–
TIMBAKI (28920)		
C	AGIOS GEORGIOS	51678
VATHIANOS KAMBOS (2810)		
C	MARILIZA	761537
VORI (28920)		
B (tr.h.)	PATRIKO	
ZAROS (28940)		
C	IDI	31301/2

LASSITHI

CATEG.	NAME	TEL.
AGIA FOTIA (28420)		
B	MARESOL	28950
C (f.a.)	ROMANZA	22600
AGIOS GEORGIOS (28440)		
E	RHEA	31209
AGIOS NIKOLAOS (28410)		
L (h.-b.)	MINOS BEACH	22345/9
L (h.-b.)	MINOS PALACE	23801/9
L (h.-b.)	MIRABELLO VILLAGE	28400/5
L	ST. NICOLAS BAY	25041/3
A (f.a.)	ALANTHA	23527
A (f.a.)	ARCHONTIKON	–
A	CRETAN VILLAGE	28576
A (f.a.)	HERA VILLAGE	28971/3
A	HERMES	28253
A	KALLITHEA	–
A (f.a.)	MAR-EGEON	25513
A (f.a.)	MARIANNA	–
A (f.a.)	MARNELOS APTS	25636
A	MIRABELLO	28400/5
A	MIRAMARE	22962
A (f.a.)	PORTO DI CANDIA-	26811
	CANDIA P. VILL	–

CATEG.	NAME	TEL.	BEDS
.)	SMARAGDI	–	22
.)	TRITON	–	24
.)	AFRODITI	28200	20
	ARIADNI BEACH	22741/3	142
	CORAL	28363/7	323
	DILINA	28292	25
	DIMITRA	23290	24
	DOMENICO	22845	46
	EL GRECO	28894	95
.)	EVITA	–	12
.)	LABYRINTH	23521	26
	MANDRAKI	28880	30
-b.)	MICRO VILLAGE	28500	133
	OLGA	22683	54
	ORMOS	24094	86
.)	RENAISSANCE	22125	44
	RHEA (Rea)	28321/3	220
	SANTA MARINA	26261/5	251
	SUNLIGHT	26622	49
	ACRATOS	22721/5	59
	ALMYROS BEACH	22865/6	95
	APOLLON	23023/5	129
.)	ARITI	24551	87
	ARTEMIS BEACH	22065	48
	ASTORIA	25148	50
	ATHINA	28225	33
.)	BELLA VISTA	–	26
	CASTLE	24918	20
.)	CHRISTINA SIDERIS	28670/1	55
.)	CRETA STAR	23845	41
	CRI-CRI	23720	32
	CRONOS	28761/2	68
	CRYSTAL	24407	74
	DILAS	28264	26
	DOXA	24214	41
	DU LAC	22711/2	60
	ELECTRA	25211/2	71
	ELENA	28189	77
	EVA	22587	12
	GEFYRA	28566	40
.)	GERANI	22551	37
.)	HAVANIA	28758	53
.)	IDRIA	23991	20
	IKAROS	28901/2	37
.)	ILIOS	–	54
	IRIS	23902	41
	KNOSSOS	24881	40
.)	KOSTIS	22717	23
	KOUROS	23264	47
	KRITI	28893/4	52
	LATO	24581/2	62
	LEVENTIS	22423	25
	LITO	23067	73
.)	LOTZIA	–	47
	MAGDA	23925	47
	MARIELLA (ex MARGIELLI)	24698	29
	MAVROFOROS	23714	25
.)	MELAS APARTMENTS	28734	31
.)	MINOAN APARTMENTS	22717	23
.)	MOUSSES	61446	31
	MYRSINI	28590	60
	NIKI	22095	20
	NIKOS	24464	73
	ODYSSEAS	23934	43
	PANGALOS	22936	43
	PANORAMA	28890	56
	POLYDOROS	22623	11

CATEG.	NAME	TEL.	BEDS
C	POSSIDONAS	24086	56
C	SGOUROS	28931	52
C	SUNRISE	23564	34
C (f.a.)	TRANTAS	–	12
C (f.a.)	TRIANA	25876	36
C	VICTORIA	22731	30
C	VLASSIS	–	90
C	ZINA	22210	35
D (f.a.)	AFROGIALIS	22109	56
D (f.a.)	ELIZA	22695	16
D (f.a.)	GALINI	24494	24
D	PERGOLA	28152	44
E	ADONIS	23379	13
E	ALMIROS RIVER	28771	39
E	ARGYRO	28707	19
E	ATLANTIS	28964	18
E	IRENE	23860	15
E	ISTRON	23763	16
E	NEW YORK	28577	16
E	PERLA	23379	15
AHLIA STAVROHORIOU (28420)			
C	GALINI	61482	47
AMMOUDARA (28410)			
B	ALCYON	24495/6	56
B (f.a.)	VIRGINIA	22782	46
C	GALINI	61482	47
C (f.a.)	DIMITRIS BEACH	–	21
C (f.a.)	MARIANTHI	28873	33
C (f.a.)	STELLA	–	29
D (f.a.)	STUDIO PIPINA	28660	60
ELOUNDA (28410)			
L (h.-b.)	ELOUNDA BAY PALACE	41502	551
L (h.-b.)	ELOUNDA BEACH	41412/3	578
L (h.-b.)	ELOUNDA MARE	41102/3	200
L	PORTO ELOUNDA RESORT	41903	413
A (f.a.)	ELOUNDA GULF VILLAS	41279	60
A	ELOUNDA ILION	41703	74
A	ELOUNDA MARMIN	41003	295
A	ELOUNDA RESIDENCE	41823	74
A (h.-b.)	GRECOTEL ELOUNDA VILLAGE	41802	316
A (tr.f.a.)	SPINALONGA VILLAGE	41494/6	34
B	DRIROS BEACH	41283	40
B	ELOUNDA BLUE BAY	41924	212
B	ELOUNDA HEIGHTS	–	18
B (f.a.)	ELOUNDA ISLAND VILLAS	41274/5	23
B	ELOUNDA PALM	41825	108
B	ESPEROS	41613	36
C	AKTI OLOUS	41270/1	95
C	ARISTEA	41300/1	62
C	CALYPSO	41367	30
C (f.a.)	KATERINA	41484	17
C	KORFOS BEACH	41591	39
C	KRINI	41602	65
C	MYRINA VILLAGE	41809	56
C	ORIZON	41895	31
C	SELENA VILLAGE	41525	128
C	SOPHIA	41482	26
C (f.a.)	TZOULAKIS	–	22
D (f.a.)	KIRKI	–	24
D	MARIA	41335	16
D (f.a.)	PALEMILOS	–	18
FERMA (28420)			
B	EDEN ROCK	61310	154
B	KAKKOS BAY	61241	79

CATEG.	NAME	TEL.	BEDS
B	PORTO BELISSARIO	61358/60	63
C (f.a.)	OASSIS	23536	26
D (f.a.)	FERMA SOLARIS	61236	29
IERAPETRA (28420)			
A	ARION PALACE	25930	129
A	ELYROS VILLAGE	61613	300
A (f.a.)	KOUTSOUNARI TRADITIONAL COTTA	–	
A	LYKTOS BEACH RESORT HOTEL	61280	432
		–	
A	PETRA MARE	23341/9	419
B	ASTRON	25114	135
B	BLUE SKY	25060/1	45
B (f.a.)	FILOXENIA	61356	28
B (f.a.)	KOTHRIS	24180	36
B (tr.f.a.)	KOUTSOUNARI HORIO NAKOU	61291	62
		–	
B	MINOAN PRINCE	25150	105
B	OSTRIA BEACH	25711/4	103
C	ACHLIA	61306	51
C	CAMIROS	28704	76
C	COSMO	25900	50
C	EL GRECO	28471/2	63
C	ERSI	23208	25
C	GALAXY	26541/3	97
C	KYRVA	22594	56
C (f.a.)	VARMY	23060	27
C	ZAKROS	24101/2	88
D	CORAL	22743	18
D	CRETAN VILLA (Kritiki Villa)	28522	18
D	IRIS	23136	21
D	IVISKOS	–	16
D	ZAFIRI	–	25
E	KASTRO KALES	23858	13
E	LIVYKON	22371	18
KALO HORIO (28410)			
L	ISTRON BAY	61303	215
A (f.a.)	KLIO	–	18
B	MISTRAL	61112	144
C	ELPIDA	61403	178
C	GOLDEN BAY	61202	94
KOUTSOUNARI IERAPETRAS (28420)			
B (h.-b.)	CORINA BEACH	61263	87
MILATOS (28410)			
D (f.a.)	PARADISE INN	81288	23
D (f.a.)	PORTO BELLO	81001	23
MIRTOS (28420)			
C	ESPERIDES	51587/8	112
C (f.a.)	MERTIZA	51208	49
C	MYRTOS	51227	32
MOHLOS (28430)			
B	ALDIANA CLUB	94211/2	262
D	SOPHIA	94554	12
E	MOHLOS	94205	15
NEAPOLIS (28410)			
C	NEAPOLIS	33966/7	21
PAHIA AMOS (28420)			
C	GOLDEN BEACH	93278	22
D	XENIOS ZEUS	93289	20
PALEKASTRO (28430)			
C (f.a.)	CASTRI VILLAGE	61100	79
C	HELLAS	61240	24
C	MARINA VILLAGE	61284	62
D (f.a.)	PORTO HELI	61275	15
D	THALIA	61448	16
E	PALEKASTRO	61235	14

CATEG.	NAME	TEL.	BEDS
PSIHRO (28440)			
D	ZEUS	31284	14
E	DICTAEON ANDRON	31504	8
E	ELENI		18
SISSI (28410)			
A	HELLENIC PALACE	71502	250
A	KALIMERA KRITI	71134	767
A	MARITIMO	71257	153
A (f.a.)	PORTO SISSI	71385/6	30
A	SISSI BAY	71298	70
A (f.a.)	SISSI MARE	71120	52
B (f.a.)	AMADEUS	–	34
B (f.a.)	CASTELLO VILLAGE I	71102	104
B (f.a.)	KOUTRAKIS APTS	–	56
B (f.a.)	MIA HARA	71702	72
C (f.a.)	ANIXI	71477	34
C (f.a.)	ANTZELA	71121	29
C (f.a.)	CASTELLO VILLAGE II	71367	97
C (f.a.)	CHRISTI-MARIE	71360	25
C	CHRISTINA-EVINA	–	82
C	ESPERIDES	–	78
C (f.a.)	SISSI BAY I	71327	22
C (f.a.)	SISSI BAY III	71298	130
C (f.a.)	SISSI ROCK	71147	115
C (f.a.)	VASSIA BEACH	71001	43
C (f.a.)	VILLES KANETOU	–	16
C (f.a.)	ZYGOS	71279	24
SITIA (28430)			
A (f.a.)	PAN MAR	51775	14
A	SITIA BEACH	28821/7	310
A (h.-b.)	SUNWING I	51621/4	315
A (f.a.)	WHITE RIVER COTTAGES	51120	21
B	SUNWING II	51621	191
B	VILLEA VILLAGE	51697	133
C	ALICE	28450	69
C	APOLLON	28155	71
C (f.a.)	ARTEMIS	51773	46
C (f.a.)	BELLE VUE	–	22
C	CASTELLO	23763	31
C	CRYSTAL	22284	75
C	DENIS	28356	25
C	EL GRECO	23133	28
C	ELYSEE	22312	49
C	GOLDEN SUN	51679	60
C	HELENA	22681	42
C	ITANOS	22900/1	138
C	MARIANA	22088	47
C (f.a.)	OKEANIDES	–	15
C	PHOENIX	28100	15
C (f.a.)	SOUTH COAST	51446	131
C (f.a.)	SUN RISE	–	16
C (f.a.)	SUNWING III	51002	192
C	VAI	22288	84
D	ARCHONTIKON	28172	22
D (f.a.)	CORINA	28320	16
D	FLISVOS	22422	19
D	MYSSON	28874	20
D	NORA	23017	16
D	STARS	22917	14
E	PETRAS BEACH	24892	18
TZERMIADO (28440)			
C	KOURITES	22194	13
E	LASSITHI	22194	14
VATHI KRITSAS (28410)			
D (f.a.)	VANGELIS	–	61
ZAKROS (28430)			
C	ZAKROS	93379	42

RETHYMNO

CATEG.	NAME	TEL.	BEDS
ADELE (28310)			
L	RETHYMNO PALACE	72418/22	318
A (h.-b.)	GRECOTEL RITHYMNA BEACH	29491	1058
B	ADELE BEACH BUNGALOWS	71081	152
B	DIAS	71017	142
B	EVA BAY	71778	159
B	GOLDEN BEACH	71012	300
B	GOLDEN SUN	71284	128
B	MARAVEL LAND	71063/4	139
B	ORION	71471/3	156
C	KATERINA BEACH	71270	194
C (f.a.)	MARAVEL	71271	110
C	RINA	71013	37
AGIA GALINI (28320)			
B	SUNNINGDALE	91161	36
C	ADONIS	91333	39
C	ADONIS II	91181	62
C	ANDROMEDA	91264	52
C	ARETI	91240	74
C	ARIADNI	91380	12
C	ASTORIA	91253	48
C	AVRA	91476	48
C	CANDIA	91203	22
C	DEDALOS	91214	24
C	EL GRECO	91187	44
C	EROFILI	91319	18
C	FEVRO	91275	97
C	GALINI MARE	91358	48
C	GHIOMA	91190	38
C	GLAROS	91151	62
C	IRINI MARE	91488	87
C	IRO	91160	31
C	NEOS IKAROS	91447	35
C	OSTRIA	91404	33
C	PETRA	91155	57
C	PORTO GALINI	91084	51
C	REA	91390	35
C	SELENA	91273	15
C	SOULIA	91307	22
C	STELLA	91357	25
C	SUN LIGHT	91286	48
D	ASTIR	91229	29
D	CRETA SUN	91123	34
D	CRISTOF	91229	29
D	IDI	91152	30
D	LETO	91231	17
D	MATHIOS	91205	23
D	MINOS	91292	23
D	PALLADA	91331	31
E	AKTAEON	91208	20
E	MICHALIS	–	21
BALI (28340)			
A (h.-b.)	BALI PARADISE	94253/4	286
B	BALI BEACH	94210/1	119
B	TALEA BEACH	94296/7	160
C	BALI MARE		89
C	BALI STAR	94155/7	120
C	BALI VILLAGE	94210	54
C (f.a.)	G. TROULIS	–	59
C (f.a.)	ORMOS ATALIA	94171	61
C	XIDAS GARDEN	94269	45
C	ZOE		33

CATEG.	NAME	TEL.
KALITHEA (28310)		
B	LEFKONIKO BEACH	55326/9
B	MINOS	53921/4
C (f.a.)	PETRIS	22465
KAMBOS PIGIS (28310)		
A	ALCYON	71136
A (h.-b.)	GRECOTEL EL GRECO	71102
B	AMNISSOS	71502
C (f.a.)	VASSIANI	
KATO RODAKINO MIRTHIOS (28320)		
B	POLYRIZOS	31334
KERATIDES PRINOU (28310)		
B	BEGIETIS BAY	71909
KOUMBES (28310)		
B (f.a.)	NIKA	25492
C (f.a.)	DELFINI	–
C	DOMICILIA	–
C (f.a.)	IRIS APARTMENTS	20114
LEFKOGIA (28320)		
C	AMMOUDI	31355/6
MASTAMBAS (28310)		
C	MARITA	26991/2
MIRTHIO (28320)		
A (f.a.)	DAMNONI RESORT	31991/3
C	DAMNONI BAY	31373
MISSIRIA (28310)		
A	GRECOTEL CRETA PALACE	55181
B (f.a.)	ANNA	22590
B (f.a.)	DOMENIKA	54475
B	MAY	55745/6
C (f.a.)	APOLLON FIVOS	24417
C (f.a.)	ARISTEA	–
C (f.a.)	EMILIA	55029
C	ODISSIA BEACH	27874
C (f.a.)	SEVEN BROTHERS	25647
D (f.a.)	KORINA	23282
D	PASSIFAE	25383
PANORMOS (28340)		
A	CRETA PANORAMA & MARE	51502
B	EUROPA	51100/1
B (f.a.)	KIRKI	51011/2
B	STELLA BEACH	51095/6
B	VILLA KYNTHIA	51102
C (f.a.)	ASTERION	51081
C (f.a.)	FILOXENIA	51481
C (f.a.)	KONAKI	51386
C	PANORMO BEACH	51321/3
D (f.a.)	KASTELI	51220/6
PERIVOLIA (28310)		
A	ATLANTIS BEACH	51002
A (f.a.)	OLYMPIC II	51527
B (f.a.)	BLUE SEA	54804/5
B (f.a.)	IRENE	24223
B (f.a.)	PEARL BEACH	51513
C	ANITA BEACH	54921
C (f.a.)	BATIS	50558
C	DIMITRIOS	–
C	ELTINA	55231/2
C (f.a.)	ERATO	26913
C (f.a.)	FLISVOS BEACH	51747
	STUDIOS	–
C (f.a.)	IVISKOS	51112
C (f.a.)	MELITI	–
C (f.a.)	MELMAR	54909
C (f.a.)	PLAZA	51505

G.	NAME	TEL.	BEDS
	SILVER BEACH	54315	108
	ZANTINA BEACH	55463/4	41
PLAKIAS (28320)			
	CALYPSO CRETIAN VILLAGE	31296/7	204
		–	
	NEOS ALIANTHOS	31280/1	173
	ALIANTHOS A'	31196	35
	FLISVOS	31421	21
	LAMON	31279	52
	LIVYKON	31216	27
	LOFOS	31422	37
	MYRTIS	31423	39
	ORIZON BEACH	31476	53
	PHOENIX	31331	34
	PLAKIAS BAY	31215	53
	SKINARIA BEACH	31295	93
	SOPHIA BEACH	31251	48
	SUDA-MARE	31931	33
PLATANES (28310)			
a.)	LEONIKI	29232	155
a.)	APP. KATERINI	54425	42
	BUENO	25554	54
	MANDENIA	27054	46
	NEFELI	55321/5	210
	RETHIMNO VILLAGE	25523	209
	SANDY BEACH	26993/4	90
a.)	STETHALI	25551/3	44
	APOLLON	–	144
.a.)	ARIADNI	54067	102
f.a.)	AXOS	23513	104
.a.)	GALEANA	54140/2	123
.a.)	MARINOS BEACH	27840	117
.a.)	PLATANES	–	75
.a.)	TRYFON	24772/4	68
.a.)	AMARIL	–	19
PLATANIAS (28310)			
.a.)	CASTELLO BIANCO	54029	86
	MINOS MARE	50388/9	135
RETHIMNO (28310)			
	ACHILLION PALACE	51502	139
	ADELE MARE	71803/8	212
	CRETA STAR	71812	591
	CRECOTEL PORTO	50432	371
	RETHYMNO	–	
r.F.a)	PALAZZO RIMONTI	51289	46
	RETHYMNO BAY	27512/3	131
	THEARTEMIS PALACE	53991	324
r.F.a)	VENETO	56634	21
r.h.)	VYZANTIO	55609	11
	ATRIUM	57601/6	247
.a.)	BELVEDERE	26898	68
	BRASCOS	23721/4	169
a.)	ELEONORA	25121/2	82
.a.)	ELINA HOLIDAYS	27395/7	44
	FILOXENIA	55345/6	71
	FORTEZZA	55551/2	102
	GORTYNA	71802	71
	IDEON	28667	160
.a.)	JASON	27196	84
	JO-AN	24241/3	113
.a.)	JOHN-MARI	51368/9	62
	KRITI BEACH	27401/2	156
	LIBERTY	55851/3	45
	MACARIS	54280/3	197
.a.)	MARDINIC	54446	38
.a.)	MYTHOS	53917	28
	OLYMPIC	24761	123

CATEG.	NAME	TEL.	BEDS
B	PANTHEON	54914	81
B (tr.h.)	RETHEMNIOTIKO SPITI	23923	19
B	RETHYMNO PANORAMA	26250	63
B (tr.h.)	VECCHIO	54985	56
B (tr.f.a.)	ZANIA	28169	12
C (tr.h.)	ADAM'S	54905	18
C (f.a.)	AMBELI	21233	14
C	ANGELOS	23702	87
C	ARCHIPELAGOS	54757	118
C (f.a.)	ARES	25382	48
C	ASTALI	24721/2	63
C (f.a.)	CAMARI GARDEN	31624	76
C (f.a.)	DAIZY	51590	45
C	FEDRA	–	23
C	FOREST PARK	51778	82
C	GREEN	22225	23
C	ILIOS	21672/4	163
C	IONIA	22902	56
C (f.a.)	KONSTANTIN	54221	46
C (f.a.)	KOSTIS	29159	46
C	KOUROS	–	39
C	KYMA BEACH	55503/4	66
C (f.a.)	LEON	26197	25
C (f.a.)	LOGGETA	27846	35
C (f.a.)	MAREM	28759	56
C (f.a.)	MERILIN	28462	48
C (tr.h.)	PALAZZO VENETIA	–	16
C	PALLADION	71789	143
C	PARK	29958	18
C (f.a.)	PIGHASSOS	25530	52
C (f.a.)	SAMARIA	53925/7	50
C	STERIS BEACH	28303	83
C (f.a.)	THEO	29769	31
C	VALARI	25140	42
C (f.a.)	VERGINA	–	45
C	ZORBAS BEACH	28540	22
D (f.a.)	AMALTHIA	23169	88
D	KASTRO	24973	20
D	MAN-MARIE	22600	31
D	MINOA	22508	57
E	AGIOS PAVLOS	41350	18
E	PARADISSOS	22419	23
E	POSSIDON	23795	23
ROUMELI MYLOPOTAMOU (28340)			
B	GRECORAMA	51070	152
SFAKAKII (28310)			
C (f.a.)	GRACE	72070	28
SFAKAKI PAGALOHORIOU (28310)			
C (f.a.)	CARETTA	72771	23
C (f.a.)	EKAVI BEACH	71896	109
SKALETA (28310)			
A	RETHYNO MARE	71703	221
B	SCALETA BEACH	71702	216
C (tr.h.)	OASSIS	71774	22
SKALETA PRINOU (28310)			
A	CRETA ROYAL	71902	224
C	BABIS	71193	30
STAVROMENOS (28310)			
C (f.a.)	ARSINIA	71283	28
C (f.a.)	ASTRID	–	30
C (f.a.)	NIKI	71038	22
C (f.a.)	PAVLOS	71304	32
D (f.a.)	LITSA-MARY	71159	26
XIROKAMARO (28310)			
C	GEORGIANNA BEACH	71503	186

CHANIA

CATEG.	NAME	TEL.	BEDS
AGIA MARINA (28210)			
A	ILIANTHOS VILLAGE	60667/8	119
B (f.a.)	ACHILLES' PARADISE	–	65
B (h.-b.)	AMALTHIA	68542	115
B	ATRION	68636,	102
B	CANEA MARE	68625	123
B	HARRIS	60173/4	87
B (f.a.)	MINERVA BEACH	68813	45
B	SANTA MARINA	68570/1	120
B	SANTA MARINA II	68460	229
B (f.a.)	SKALA	68680	16
C (f.a.)	ACITION	68692	59
C	ALEXIA BEACH	68110/1	41
C (f.a.)	ANTIGONE	68109	23
C	APELIA	60410	38
C (f.a.)	APLADAS	68700/3	132
C (f.a.)	ARCHITECT'S VILLAS II	68526	18
C (f.a.)	ATLANTIDA MARE	60966	31
C	ATRION VILLAGE	68636	93
C	BELLA VISTA VILLAGE	68100	50
C (f.a.)	EL-MA	–	32
C (f.a.)	ELOTIS	68622	52
C (f.a.)	EROFILI	68529	33
C (f.a.)	IOLIDA	68776/7	91
C (f.a.)	MANIAS	60288	31
C	MARINA SANDS	68691/3	70
C (f.a.)	MARRIOT VILLAGE	60751	119
C	MEGAS ALEXANDROS	60061	25
C	MIMOZA	60614	46
C (f.a.)	NINEMIA	68983	21
C (f.a.)	OSCAR	68773	99
C (f.a.)	RELAX	68806	118
C (f.a.)	SEA-GULL	68747	68
C (f.a.)	STEFAN OLIVE GROVE	68130	97
C (f.a.)	STEFAN VILLAGE	68130	90
C	TA THODOROU	68510	32
C	THEO	60960	80
C (f.a.)	TROULIS	–	53
C (f.a.)	VERGINA	60052	33
D (f.a.)	EVANGELINA	68420	48
AGIA ROUMELI (28250)			
C	AGHIA ROUMELI	91232	13
C	CRI-CRI	–	24
AGII APOSTOLOI (28210)			
C (f.a.)	CALYPSO	32013	64
C (f.a.)	CRETA DREAM	32170	95
C (f.a.)	FLAMINGOS	32046	72
D (f.a.)	NIRIIS	33012	33
ALMIRIDA (28250)			
A	DIMITRA	31956	70
B	ALMIRIDA BAY	31751	93
C (f.a.)	ALMIRA	–	14
C (f.a.)	NIRIIDES	32450	33
ASPROULIANOS GEORGIOUPOLIS (28250)			
C (f.a.)	VARDIS	61334	47
DARATSOS (28210)			
A (f.a.)	STAR DARATSOS	32291	38
B (b.)	ALTHEA VILLAGE	31320	120
B (f.a.)	GOLDEN BAY	32802	76
B (f.a.)	KARAVANOS	32315	23
B (f.a.)	MALOU	32332	24
B	SIRIOS VILLAGE	32102	359
C	AMMOS	33003	66
C (f.a.)	ASTRA	32302	29
C (f.a.)	CLEO	32326	28

CATEG.	NAME	TEL.	BEDS
C (f.a.)	DREAM LAND	32379	51
C (f.a.)	GOLDEN SAND	32351/3	66
C (f.a.)	LOTUS	31660	46
C (f.a.)	NANA	32553	40
C (f.a.)	TALOS	32050	34

DARATSOS (KATO) (28210)

CATEG.	NAME	TEL.	BEDS
C (f.a.)	MEDITERRANEAN	33234	94
C (f.a.)	REIZAKIS	32786	31

DRAMIA (28310)

CATEG.	NAME	TEL.	BEDS
B	PORTO GEORGIOUPOLI	61702/4	151
C	MARI	61569	90

ELOS VATHI (28220)

CATEG.	NAME	TEL.	BEDS
C	AGIOS DIKAEOS	61275	17

FYLAKI APOKORONOU (28310)

CATEG.	NAME	TEL.	BEDS
C	ERMIONI	61678/9	56

GALATAS (28210)

CATEG.	NAME	TEL.	BEDS
A	PANORAMA	96700	309
C (f.a.)	BALITO	–	41
C	DAFNI	46632	50
C (f.a.)	GIANNIS-ELENI	31866	46
C (f.a.)	KORINNA	31767	28
C	VACHOS	31711	44
C (f.a.)	VENUS	32110	17
C (f.a.)	VILLA ANASTASIA	31413	20
C (f.a.)	VILLA ARMONIA	31946	18
C (f.a.)	ZOTIS	32413	34

GEORGIOUPOLI (28250)

CATEG.	NAME	TEL.	BEDS
A	ELIROS BEACH	61181	114
A	MARE MONTE	61390	195
A	PILOT BEACH	61002/3	194
A	VANTARIS BEACH	61006	102
B	DELFINA BEACH	61272	101
B	GEORGIOUPOLIS BEACH	–	98
C (f.a.)	AFRODITI	61595	34
C	DROSSIA	61326	23
C (f.a.)	E.K.O.	61493	35
C	GORGONA	61341	79
C	KORISSIA	61389	82
C	LAVYRINTHOS	61373	42
C	MITHOLOGY	61414	59
C (f.a.)	NIKITAS	61283	14
C (f.a.)	NOSTALGIE	61400	63
C (f.a.)	PAPADAKIS	61618	63
C (f.a.)	TARRA	–	30
E	ALMYROS	61349	13
E	AMPHIMALA	61362	18
E	NIKOLAS	61375	33
E	PENELOPE	61370	33
E	ZORBAS	61381	42

GERANI (28210)

CATEG.	NAME	TEL.	BEDS
A	CRETA PARADISE BEACH	61315	184
B	CRETA PARADISE	61190	184
C (f.a.)	IANTHIA	61205	81
C (f.a.)	KOSTAKIS BEACH	61619	90
C (f.a.)	PROIMOS APTS. GERANI	61126	41
C (f.a.)	SILVER BEACH	61668	65

GERMANIKO POULI (28210)

CATEG.	NAME	TEL.	BEDS
C (f.a.)	AGAPI	27410	17

HALEPA (28210)

CATEG.	NAME	TEL.	BEDS
B	ROYAL SUN	42618	42

HANIA (28210)

CATEG.	NAME	TEL.	BEDS
A (tr.h.)	AMFORA	93224	42
A (tr.h.)	BOZZALI	50525/6	15
A (tr.h.)	CAPTAIN VASSILIS	94033	13
A (tr.h.)	CONTESSA	98565/6	14
A (tr.f.a.)	DOGIS	95466	18
A	KYDON	52280/4	191
A (tr.h.)	PALAZZO	93227	25
A (tr.f.a.)	PANDORA	43588/9	28
A (tr.h.)	PORTO DEL COLOMBO	70945	20
B	AKALI MELATHRON	92872/6	152
B	ARCADI	90181	114
B (tr.f.a.)	CASA DELFINO	93098	31
B (f.a.)	CASA VENETA	90007	23
B	DOLPHIN II APARTMENTS	93481	38
B	DOMA	51772/3	48
B	DOMENICO	55019	10
B (tr.h.)	EL GRECO	90432	25
B	ELENA	95516	13
B (tr.h.)	HALEPA	28440	94
B (f.a.)	ILIANTHOS	20828	11
B (f.a.)	KAROLOS STUDIOS	55019	6
B (tr.h.)	MARILY	95589	9
B	MINOA	27970	41
B	MONTE VARDIA	45444	38
B (tr.h.)	NOSTOS	94740	27
B (f.a.)	NOTOS	–	64
B (tr.h.)	PASIPHAE	–	15
B	PORTO VENEZIANO	27100	108
B	RODON	58317/8	60
B	SAMARIA	71271/5	117
B (tr.f.a.)	VILLA ANDROMEDA	28300/1	24
B	XENIA	91238/9	88
C	AKROTIRI	54669	26
C	AMPHITRITI	56470/1	26
C (f.a.)	ARIS	–	21
C	ARTEMIS	23035	10
C	ASTOR	55557/8	68
C	CANDIA	91943	33
C	CANEA	91360/2	94
C (f.a.)	CASA LEONE	56372	12
C (f.a.)	CRETA HELENA	43722/3	45
C	DANAOS	96021/2	57
C	DIKTYNNA	51145	61
C	ELOTIA	32651	59
C	FALASSARNA	93736/8	56
C	FALIRO	41904/5	17
C	HELLINIS	51850	59
C	IRENE	94667	39
C	IRIDA	46060	33
C	KRITI	51881/5	189
C	KYDONIA	95343/5	68
C	LATO	95088	51
C (f.a.)	LIVA	45310/1	41
C	LUCIA	90302/3	72
C (tr.f.a.)	MADONA	94747	11
C	NEFELI	70007	65
C	OMALOS	95215/7	63
C	POSSIDONIO	87404	23
C	ZEPOS	44921/2	34
D (f.a.)	LEFKA ORI	90684	25
D	THEOFILOS	53294	30
D	TINA	41195	26
E	AFRODITI	57602	20
E	ALEDANDROS (ex Manos)	94284	19
E	ARIADNE	–	19
E	AVEROF	90808	20
E	FRYNI	21518	59
E	MONASTIRI	54776	16
E	PHEDIAS	52494	43
E	VIENNOS	90555	18

HRYSSI AKTI KYDONIAS (28210)

CATEG.	NAME	TEL.
C (f.a.)	ANAIS HOLIDAY	33300/1
C (f.a.)	ELMA'S DREAM	87401
C (f.a.)	GOLDEN SUN	–
C (f.a.)	TRITON	87003/5

KALAMAKI (28210)

CATEG.	NAME	TEL.
C	AKASTI	31352
C	ALEXANDRA	32055
C	ARIADNI	31620/3

KALATHAS (AKROTIRI) (28210)

CATEG.	NAME	TEL.
B	GIORGI'S BLUE APTS	64080
B	LENA-AKTI	64750/1
B (f.a.)	WATER LILY	64755
C (f.a.)	AREA	69002
C (f.a.)	ARION	64637
C (f.a.)	ESPLANADE	64253
C (f.a.)	KRINI	64795
C (f.a.)	SUNRISE	64214
C	TZANAKAKI BEACH	64363/5
D (f.a.)	VILLA FERENIKI	64073

KALIVES (28250)

CATEG.	NAME	TEL.
B (f.a.)	MAISTRALI	31902
C	KALIVES BEACH	31285

KAMISSIANA (28240)

CATEG.	NAME	TEL.
B (f.a.)	KASTALIA	22268
C (f.a.)	DIOM'S STUDIOS	22376

KANDANOS (28230)

CATEG.	NAME	TEL.
C (f.a.)	APOPIGADI	22566/7

KATO GALATAS (28210)

CATEG.	NAME	TEL.
C (f.a.)	VIGLA	32770

KATO GERANI (28210)

CATEG.	NAME	TEL.
C (f.a.)	ALFA	61112

KATO STALOS (28210)

CATEG.	NAME	TEL.
C (f.a.)	AEGLI	–
C	ALCYON	68022
C	ANNIKO	–
C (f.a.)	ATLANTIS BEACH	68537
C (f.a.)	CASA LOMA	60686
C (f.a.)	CLEOPATRA	60729
C (f.a.)	CRYSTAL	60715/6
C	DOLFIN	68507
C (f.a.)	ESPERIDES	68672
C (f.a.)	EVILION	68196
C (f.a.)	KATO STALOS	68120/1
C (f.a.)	KOUKOURAS	–
C (f.a.)	KOURMOULIS STUDIOS	68804
C (f.a.)	PAVLAKIS BEACH	68309
C (f.a.)	SEA SIDE	68778
C (f.a.)	TROPIKANA BEACH	68787
D (f.a.)	EVA	68010

KAVROS (28250)

CATEG.	NAME	TEL.
B	KOURNAS VILLAGE	61416/2
C	ANATOLI	61001
C	HAPPY DAYS BEACH	61201/2
C	ORFEAS BEACH	61008
C	SOFIA	–

KASTELLI (KISSAMOS) (28220)

CATEG.	NAME	TEL.
B	HELENA BEACH	23300/4
B	HERMES	24109
C	ADELAIS	–
C	ASTRIKAS	–
C	CASTLE	22140/1
C (f.a.)	DELFINI	23390
C (f.a.)	DIMITRIS-CHRYSSANI	22337
C	HOLIDAYS	23488
C	KISSAMOS	22086
C	PELI	23223

G.	NAME	TEL.	BEDS
.a.)	PERGAMOS VILLAGE	22944/5	60
	VAI	22790	22
.a.)	MANDY	22825	27
	KOLIMBARI (28240)		
.r.f.a.)	DIKTINNA	–	26
.a.)	APHAEA VILLAGE	23344/5	72
	ARION	22440	38
	CHRYSSANA	22812	78
.a.)	AEOLOS	22203	28
	KOLYMBARI BEACH	22725	146
.a.)	LYKASTI	22822	63
	NIRIIDES	22257	55
	DIMITRA	22244	48
	KORAKIES (28210)		
	CORAKIES VILLAGE	64584	34
	KOUNOUPIDIANA (28210)		
f.a.)	LEONIDAS	64472	32
	PYRGOS	64431	31
f.a.)	TARSANAS	39277	60
	KOURNA (28250)		
	KAVROS BEACH	61322	202
	MANOS BEACH	61221	30
	SILVER BEACH	61223	15
	MAKRIS TICHOS (28210)		
f.a.)	THEOS VILLAGE	87150/2	65
f.a.)	NIKOLAS	32105	39
	MALEME (28210)		
h.-b.)	LOUIS CRETA PRINCESS	62221/6,	767
	ALBATROS	–	62
f.a.)	ALEXANDROS M	62653	45
f.a.)	ARADIN	–	17
	BELLA PAIS	62732	63
f.a.)	FLISVOS	62188	39
f.a.)	FUTURA	62610/1	84
f.a.)	LEDRA	62366	34
f.a.)	LEDRA MALEME	62042	35
f.a.)	MALEME MARE	62121	90
	EL-KI	62490	22
	METOHI KISSAMOU (28220)		
f.a.)	VIGLIA BEACH	–	92
	NEA KIDONIA (28210)		
f.a.)	ANAIS	33300/1	32

CATEG.	NAME	TEL.	BEDS
B	KIRIAKI	87910/1	44
C	ALEXIS	93733/4	50
C (f.a.)	FORUM	32425	106
C (f.a.)	GOLDEN BEACH	32128	18
C	KEDRISSOS	71500	47
C (f.a.)	KORINNA MARE	31767	57
C (f.a.)	RAINBOW	32002	34
C (f.a.)	STELLINA VILLAGE	32178	52
	OMALOS (28210)		
C	NEOS OMALOS	67269	49
C	TO EXARI	67180	46
	PALEOCHORA (28230)		
B (f.a.)	ELMAN	41412/4	41
C	AGHAS	41155	31
C	ARIS	41502	56
C	DICTAMO	41569	33
C	GLAROS	41613	29
C	MEGIM	41690	44
C (f.a.)	NIKOLAS	41165	20
C	ON THE ROKS	41713	22
C	PAL BEACH	41512	104
C	POLYDOROS	41150	24
C	REA	41307	27
E	LISSOS	41266	21
E	OASSIS	41328	22
E	POSEIDON	41374	31
	PERIVOLIA (28210)		
C	OASSIS	94829	56
	PLAKA APOKORONOU (28250)		
B (f.a.)	EMERALD	31753	22
	PLATANIAS (28210)		
B	GERANIOTIS BEACH	68681	150
B	IDEAL BEACH	–	110
B (f.a.)	RITA	60281	78
B	SANTA ELENA	68767	244
C (f.a.)	ANNA-MARIA	–	23
C	ARCHIPELAGOS	–	46
C (f.a.)	CASA CAMARA	–	45
C (f.a.)	DESPINA	68807	59
C (f.a.)	ELISSO VILLAGE	60930	60
C (f.a.)	ERATO	68824	157
C (f.a.)	ERMIS	60101	30
C (f.a.)	EVROPI	60519	31

CATEG.	NAME	TEL.	BEDS
C	FILOXENIA	68502	18
C (f.a.)	GIASSEMOCHORI IVISKOS	68060	126
C (f.a.)	GIASSEMOCHORI LYDIA	68060	151
C (f.a.)	GIASSEMOCHORI MYRIA	68060	126
C (f.a.)	GIASSEMOCHORI OLEA	68060	82
C (f.a.)	IFIGENIA	–	18
C (f.a.)	INDIGO MARE	68156	101
C (f.a.)	KALLIA	60280/2	24
C (f.a.)	KASTRO	48583	99
C (f.a.)	KRONOS	68630/2	99
C (f.a.)	MARAKIS	–	25
C (f.a.)	MARIKA	–	41
C (f.a.)	RANIA	–	38
C (f.a.)	VAROUXAKIS	–	57
C	VILLA PLATANIAS	48333	20
D (f.a.)	AGAPI	68106	33
	PLATANIAS ANO (28210)		
C (f.a.)	MYTHOS	60864	27
	PYRGOS PSILOMENOU (28210)		
A	AEGEAN	62668	100
C (f.a.)	BELLE HELENE	62604	12
C (f.a.)	OLGA	62776	45
	RAPANIANA KISSAMOU (28240)		
B	KRISPI	22966	112
C	SEA VIEW	22213	64
	SFAKIA (28250)		
B	VRITOMARTIS	91112	161
C	PORTO LOUTRO	91444	49
C	XENIA	91238	23
	SOUDA (28210)		
D	KNOSSOS	81230	17
D	PARTHENON	89245	13.
	SOUGIA (28230)		
C	PIKILASSOS	51242	19
C (f.a.)	SANTA IRENE	51342	30
	STALOS (28210)		
C (f.a.)	IRINI	60681	25
	STAVROS (AKROTIRI) (28210)		
B	ELEANA	39480	33
B	REA	39001/4	74
	VAMOS (28250)		
B (tr.h.)	THE OLD GIRL'S SCHOOL	22266	21

CAMPING

PREFECTURE	TEL.
CHANIA	
CHANIA (28210)	
Apostoli	33138, 34203
KISSAMOS (28220)	
...samos, Kasteli	23444
MYTHIMNA (28220)	
...panias, Kissamou	31444/5
NOPIGIA (28210)	
...samos	31111
PALEOCHORA (28230)	
...eochora	41120

PREFECTURE	TEL.
RETHYMNO	
AGIA GALINI (28320)	
Agia Galini	91386
APOLLONIA (28320)	
Plakias	31507
ELIZABETH (28310)	
Missiria, Rethimno	28694

PREFECTURE	TEL.
IRAKLIO	
CARAVAN (28970)	
Limenas Hersonissou	22025
CRETA (28970)	
Gouves Hersonissou	41400
HERSONISSOS (28970)	
Anissaras	22902
KOMOS (28920)	
Komos Pitsidion	42596
MATALA (28920)	
Matala	42340

PREFECTURE	TEL.
LASSITHI	
GOURNIA MOON (28420)	
Gournia, Ag. Nikolaos	93243
KOUTSOUNARI (28420)	
Koutsounari, Ierapetra	61213
SISSI (28410)	
Sissi, Mirabelou	71247

INDEX CHANIA

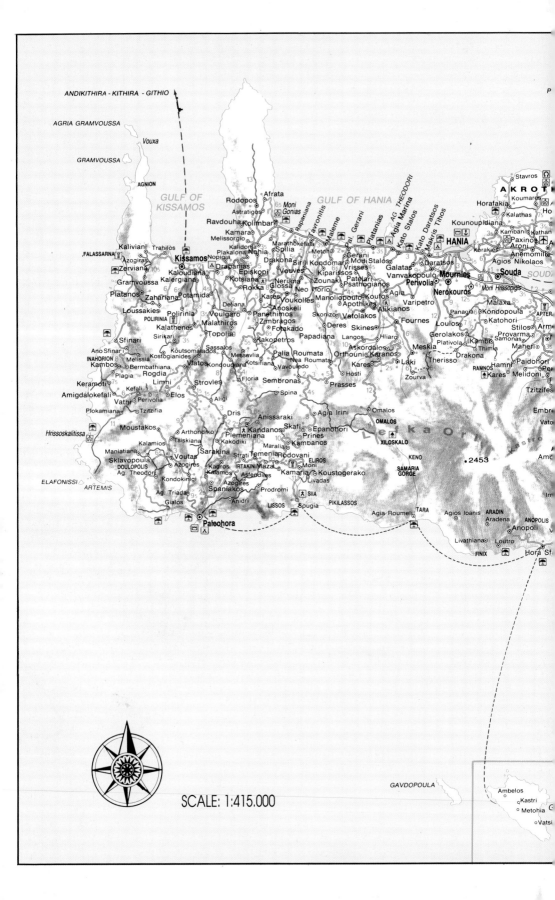

PIREAS PIREAS

Stavros

ALMIROS BAY

Lavris Panormos
Roumeli Skepasti Bali
exandrou Ahlades Exandis Agios Ahláda
Amigdali AMFIMALA Prinos Angeliana Melidoni Koanias Moni Fodele Moni Sava
orgioupoli IDRAMIA Perama Koulo Ag. Pandeleimonas Ro
Petres RETHIMNO Pervolia Missiria Ilani Alexandrou Alfa Agia Aloides Damasta Marathos
thes Gerani Platanes Arsenlou Asteri Erfi Plevriana Dafnedes Apladiana Doxaro Theodora Drossia Met. K.
Mouri Fr. Prines Galos Adele Pigi Loutra Pikris Skoulofia Margarites Orthes Episkopi Garazo Moni Halepas Honos Astiraki
Kastelos Metohia Maroulas Messa Kiriana Ammatos Eleftherna Prines Avdelas Agios Ioanis Veni Aimonas Aidonohori Kamariotis Tilis
nas Kouri Somatas Gonia Hromonastiri Prassies Kavoussi Agios Mamas Kalivos Axos Diakouri Gonies TILISS
Patima Aihondiki Kastelos Armeni Mirthios Harkia Arkadi ELEFTHERNA Krana Livadia Sissarha SKLAVOKAMBOS
Zourid Ag. Ano Oros Voleones SIVRITOS Klissidi Zoniana Anogia Kama
Argiroupoli Kons/nos Roustika Kare Goulediana Thronos Korfes
lia Poros Malaki Fotinos Genf Pandanassa Agia Fotini Vistagi Loutraki
Moundros Saitoures Koumi Karines Patsos Meronas Moni Assomaton Platania Kroussonas
Miriokefala Arolithi Vilandredo Agios Kali Sikia Agios Apostoli Amari Monastiraki 2456 IDEON CAVE Moni Gorgolaini Sar
atis Alones Vassilios Ioanis Lambini Messonissi Elenes Lambiotes Fourfouras NIDA Kato Assites
kaloti Ano Angousseliana Atsipades Koxare Dariviana Vrisses Petrohori Vizari Kouroutes Pano Assites
Rodakino Mariou Spili Gerakaki Drigies Ano Meros Nithavris KAMARES RIZINI
Argoules Kato Selia Mixorooma Kissos Kambos Kendrohori Agios CAVE Prinias
Plakias Mirthios Assomatos Aktounda Vatos Platanes Ioanis Lohria Kamares Moni Vrondissi
Lefkogia Drimiskos Kerames Vrisses Ardaktos Hordak Platanos Vorizia Gergeri Ag.
Gianiou K.M. Akoumia Kria Vrissi Ardaktos Moni Nivritos Panassos
Moni Preveli Preveli Agalianos Agia Paraskevi Vathiako Grigoria Varsamonerou Zaros Apomarma
Siderotas 1136 Orne Apodoulou Rizikas Magarikari Kardamiana Makres
Ag. Paraskevi K. Saktouria Mandres Sata Klima Kalohorafitis Lalounas Raptis
Melambes Klima Skourvoula Plouti Vourvoulitis
Ag. Pavlos Saktouria Xerokambos Lagoli Kissi Moroni GORTIS
Agia Galini Faneromeni Galia Roufas Ambelouzos Agii Deka
Kok. Prigos Vori Kaliviani Kastell Mitropoli Gan
Timbaki Kamilari Houstouliana
MESSARAS BAY Kalamaki AGIA TRIAS FESTOS Mires Petrokefali Peri Platanos Vag
PAXIMADIA Pitsidia Sivas Kousses Alithini Plora Vassilika
KOMO Listaros Pombia Agia Marina Anogia
Matala MATALA Pigaidakia Agios Kirilos Vassi
Moni Odigitrias Moni Miamou Vassi
Apezanon Krotos
LASSEA Andiskari LEVIN
Kali Limenes Pl. Peramata Lendas
Lithino Papadogianis

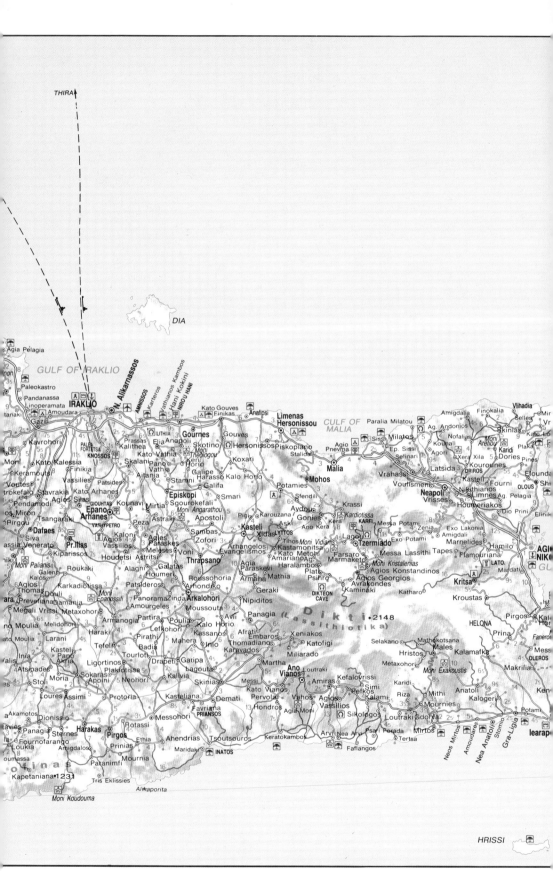

THIRA

DIA

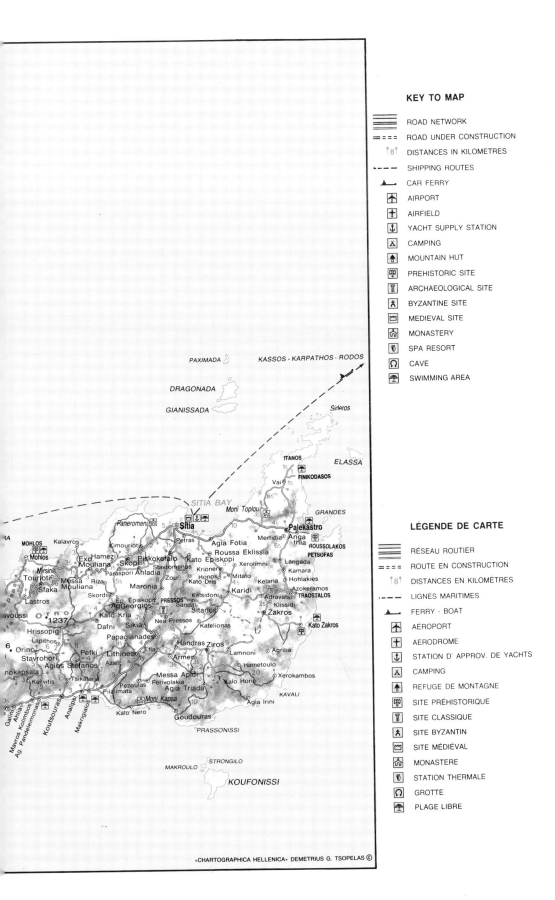

TOWN PLAN OF CHANIA

PUBLIC BUILDINGS AND SERVICES
1. TOWN HALL - PUBLIC LIBRARY
2. PREFECTURE
3. NATIONAL TOURIST ORGANIZATION
   OFFICES (1645 MOSQUE)
4. TOURIST POLICE
5. CUSTOMS OFFICE

6. COURTS OF LAW
7. HOSPITAL
8. POST OFFICE
9. TELEPHONE COMPANY (OTE)
10. OLYMPIC AIRWAYS OFFICES
11. ELPA (AUTOMOBILE ASSOCIATION)

PLACES OF INTEREST
12. ''FIRKAS'' FORTRESS - NAVAL MUSEUM

13. VENETIAN LIGHTHOUSE
14. VENETIAN SHIPYARDS
15. SCHIAVO, OR LANDO BAST
16. CATHEDRAL
17. SAINT ROCCO CHURCH
18. CHURCH OF SAINT NICHOL
19. CHURCH OF AGHIOI ANARC
20. RENIERI GATE
21. ARCHAEOLOGICAL MUSEU

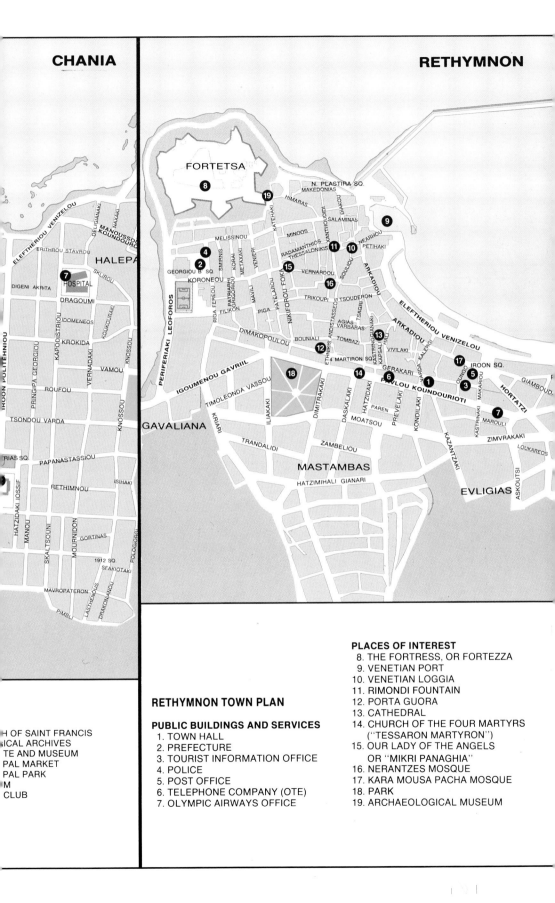

CHANIA

RETHYMNON

FORTETSA

HALEPA

ELEFTHERIOU VENIZELOU
DELIGIANNI
MANOUSSO
KOUNDOURO
NAXAKI
ERITHROU STAVROU
SKLIROU
DIGENI AKRITA
HOSPITAL
DRAGOUMI
KAPODISTRIOU
IDOMENEOS
KROKIDA
KOUKOURAKI
KNOSSOU
VERNADAKI
VAMOU
PRINGIPA GEORGIOU
ROUFOU
TSONDOU VARDA
RIAS SQ.
PAPANASTASSIOU
ISIHAKI
RETHIMNOU
HATZIDAKI IOSSIF
MANOU
SKALTSOUNI
MOURNIDON
GORTINAS
POLOGIORGI
1912 SQ.
SEAFIOTAKI
MAVROPATERON
LASTHENOUS
DRAKONAKOU
PIMBLI

IROON POLITEHNIOU
PERIFERIAKI LEOFOROS

MELISSINOU
GEORGIOU B SQ.
KORONEOU
RIGA FEREOU
PATRIARHI GRIGORIOU
FILIKON
PIGA
SMIRNIS
KORAI
METAXAKI
MAVILI
PATELAROU
NIKIFOROU FOKA
DIMAKOPOULOU
IGOUMENOU GAVRIIL
TIMOLEONDA VASSOU
KRIARI
ILIAKAKI
GAVALIANA
TRANDALIDI
ZAMBELIOU
MASTAMBAS
HATZIMIHALI GIANARI

N. PLASTIRA SQ.
MAKEDONIAS
HIMARAS
KATEHAKI
MINOOS
DHAVID
SALAMINAS
VENIERI
RADAMANTHIOS
THESSALONIKIS XANTHOUDIDI
VERNARDOU
NEARHOU
PETIHAKI
SOULIOU
ARKADIOU
TRIKOUPI TSOUDERON
AGIAS VARBARAS
ETHNIKIS ANDISTASSEOS
BOUNIALI
TOMBAZI
4 MARTIRON
KASTRINOGIANAKI
KAPSALI
KARAOLI
VIVILAKI
GERAKARI
PAVLOU KOUNDOURIOTI
DASKALAKI
HATZIDAKI
PAREN
PREVELAKI
KONDILAKI
MOATSOU
KAZAN TZAKI
KASTRINAKI MAKARIOU
IROON SQ.
HORTATZI
MAROULI
ZIMVRAKAKI
LOUKAREOS
ASKOUTSI
GIAMBOUD.
EVLIGIAS
ELEFTHERIOU VENIZELOU
ARKADIOU
OUNDO KALERGI

H OF SAINT FRANCIS
ICAL ARCHIVES
TE AND MUSEUM
PAL MARKET
PAL PARK
M
CLUB

RETHYMNON TOWN PLAN

PUBLIC BUILDINGS AND SERVICES
1. TOWN HALL
2. PREFECTURE
3. TOURIST INFORMATION OFFICE
4. POLICE
5. POST OFFICE
6. TELEPHONE COMPANY (OTE)
7. OLYMPIC AIRWAYS OFFICE

PLACES OF INTEREST
8. THE FORTRESS, OR FORTEZZA
9. VENETIAN PORT
10. VENETIAN LOGGIA
11. RIMONDI FOUNTAIN
12. PORTA GUORA
13. CATHEDRAL
14. CHURCH OF THE FOUR MARTYRS ("TESSARON MARTYRON")
15. OUR LADY OF THE ANGELS OR "MIKRI PANAGHIA"
16. NERANTZES MOSQUE
17. KARA MOUSA PACHA MOSQUE
18. PARK
19. ARCHAEOLOGICAL MUSEUM

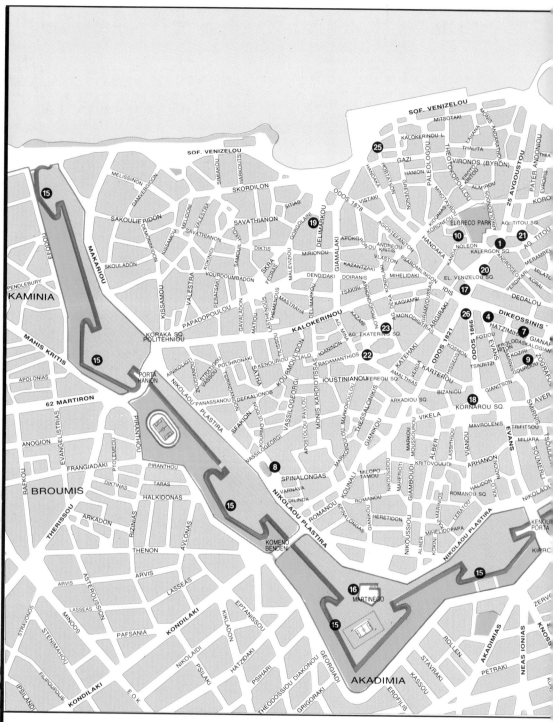

HERAKLEION TOWN PLAN

PUBLIC BUILDINGS AND SERVICES
1. VENETIAN LOGGIA - TOWN HALL
2. PREFECTURE
3. NATIONAL TOURIST
   ORGANIZATION OFFICES
4. TOURIST POLICE
5. HARBOURMASTER'S OFFICE

6. CUSTOMS OFFICE
7. COURTS OF LAW
8. HOSPITAL
9. POST OFFICE
10. TELEPHONE COMPANY (OTE)
11. KTEL BUS STATION
12. OLYMPIC AIRWAYS OFFICE
13. ELPA (AUTOMOBILE
    ASSOCIATION)

PLACES OF INTEREST
14. KOULES
15. BASTIONS OF THE VENETIAN WALLS
16. KAZANTZAKIS' GRAVE
17. MOROSINI FOUNTAIN
18. BEMBO FOUNTAIN
19. PRIULI OR DELIMARCOS FOUNTAIN
20. BASILICA OF SAINT MARK
21. CHURCH OF ST. TITUS

HERAKLEION

AGHIOS NIKOLAOS

AGHIOS NIKOLAOS TOWN PLAN

PUBLIC BUILDINGS AND SERVICES
1. TOWN HALL - LIBRARY
2. PREFECTURE
3. TOURIST POLICE
   TOURIST INFORMATION
4. HARBOURMASTER'S OFFICE -
   FOLK ART MUSEUM
5. POST OFFICE
6. TELEPHONE COMPANY (OTE)

7. HOSPITAL
8. OLYMPIC AIRWAYS OFFICE

PLACES OF INTEREST
9. CHURCH OF AGHIA TRIADA -
   CATHEDRAL
10. ARCHAEOLOGICAL MUSEUM
11. VOULISMENI LAKE

URCH OF ST. MINAS -
THEDRAL
HIA AIKATERINI
LLECTION OF BYZANTINE
ONS
CHAEOLOGICAL MUSEUM
STORICAL MUSEUM
NICIPAL MARKET

PRODUCTION - PRINTING - BINDING: **PERGAMOS PRINTING & PUBLISHING S.A.**